To my dearest MA ♥ Nancy Alden

A TOUCH
OF GLASS

DESIGNS FOR CREATING GLASS BEAD JEWELRY

NANCY ALDEN
COFOUNDER OF BEADWORKS

A TOUCH
OF GLASS

DESIGNS FOR CREATING GLASS BEAD JEWELRY

POTTER
CRAFT

NEW YORK

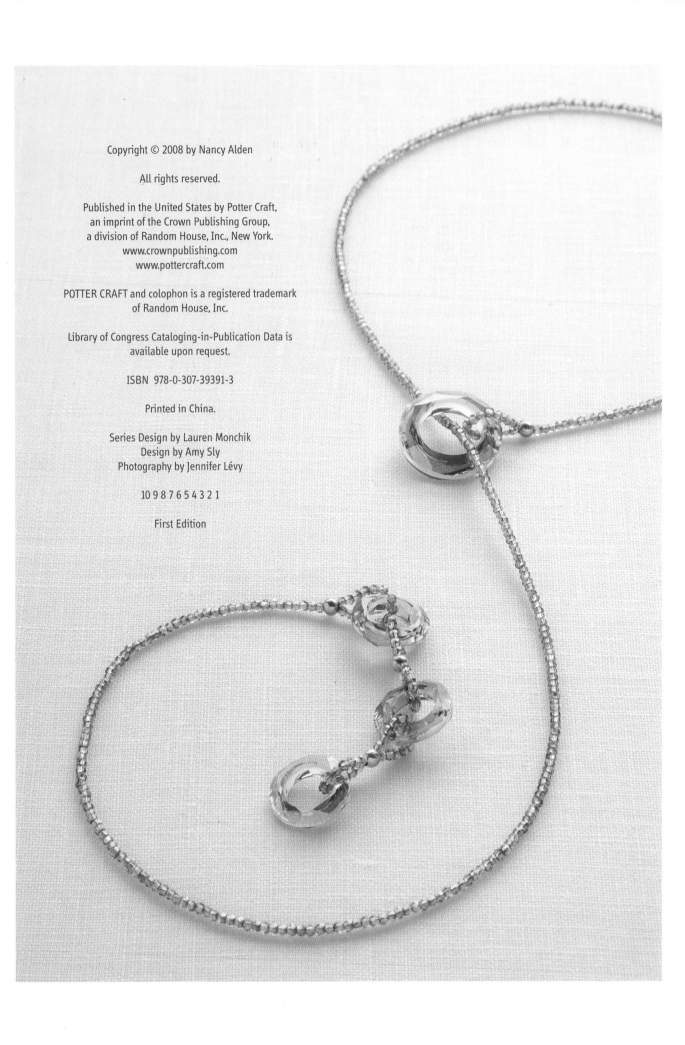

Published in the United States by Potter Craft,
an imprint of the Crown Publishing Group,
a division of Random House, Inc., New York.
www.crownpublishing.com
www.pottercraft.com

POTTER CRAFT and colophon is a registered trademark
of Random House, Inc.

Library of Congress Cataloging-in-Publication Data is
available upon request.

ISBN 978-0-307-39391-3

Printed in China.

Series Design by Lauren Monchik
Design by Amy Sly
Photography by Jennifer Lévy

10 9 8 7 6 5 4 3 2 1

First Edition

CONTENTS

INTRODUCTION

Though I have spent much of my life making jewelry with precious metals and stones, I am filled with great appreciation and admiration for the simple virtues of glass. When silver and gold prices rose to heights neither I nor my clients could reach, I turned to glass, seeking economy and found a wonderful world of affordable "jewels" that has fascinated me ever since. Glass may be a common and modest material, but when it is transformed by talent and skill, it occupies an important position on the jeweler's palette.

As a large-scale buyer of jewelry components, I have learned a lot about the production of glass beads and been privileged to meet many talented artisans. I have watched them painstakingly build their small works of art in front of an open flame, and I have worked with them to design entirely new beads. In small cottages of northern Bohemia and canal-side workshops of Venice, I have seen drops of molten glass shaped on thin metal rods by skilled, patient women. I have even learned to use the torch myself and had the immense satisfaction of seeing a new, if slightly clumsy and misshapen, bead take shape under my own hands. In the Czech Republic, Japan, China, and India, I have observed the larger-scale production of beads: some in peaceful rooms with gently humming high-tech equipment, others in steamy factories filled with hot furnaces, boisterous machinery, and noisome baths of dyes and glazes.

Glass beads can enchant viewers with a particular hue imitating a fine gem or with a unique color that challenges anything found in nature. They can be an abstract collage of tones, textures, and glitter that dazzles the eye or miniature masterpieces of sculpture and three-dimensional painting.

In this book, we'll explore the major categories of glass beads and show what each kind can offer to your own designs—whether you are seeking simplicity and economy or complexity and high value. In the jewelry designer's constant search for the novel and for yet another way to delight the eye, it is glass that so often provides the answer.

GLASS BEAD BASICS

HISTORY OF GLASS BEADS

Beads are the oldest known objects of body decoration. The earliest beads—simple shells with pierced holes—have been dated to almost 100,000 years ago. While "natural" beads, such as shells and pearls, predate man-made materials by tens of thousands of years, glass beads are surprisingly ancient and encompass enough history to embrace most of human civilization. For a jewelry designer, it is an added pleasure to be a part of such a long tradition, as well as know the historical highlights in the story of glass beads.

The oldest true glass beads from ancient Egypt and Mesopotamia are around 3,500 years old. Forerunners to true glass, like Egyptian faience (a glazed earthenware material) and glazed steatite (soapstone), carry the beginnings of glass beads more than 2,000 years further back into history. While the techniques for glass-making were well known in ancient times, it was in the fourth century B.C. that the unbroken tradition of fine glass bead-making really began. The city of Alexandria became the cosmopolitan center of Egypt, providing an outlet for exporting glass-working skills across the Mediterranean to Greece, to Phoenicia, and, most importantly, to Rome.

It was the Roman Empire that began the great global trade of glass beads. During the period from 100 B.C. to 400 A.D., many advances were made in both the production of raw glass and the techniques used to shape it into beautiful objects. An extensive glass industry developed throughout the Roman Empire, and glass beads were a major part of its production. Factories blossomed from the Syrian deserts to the banks of the Rhine, and trading routes carried glass beads to the far reaches of the Empire and beyond to China, Scandinavia, and Central Africa. By the time the Roman Empire started to fall apart, the global desire for glass beads had been firmly established.

The decline of the Roman Empire, however, led to a sharp drop in the production of glass beads. Consequently, workshops in other parts of the world, particularly in India, stepped in to supply the glass bead trade, shipping their products on all the maritime trading routes. China and Japan, each having a long tradition of glass bead-making, continued to supply their own markets in Asia.

During the Middle Ages, glass bead-making continued in various locations of the former Roman lands, sometimes in small workshops and often as a cottage industry. However, it was up to the Venetians to rediscover many of the more sophisticated Roman techniques, as well as to re-establish a glass bead-making industry on a major scale—one that was to find a place among the other vibrant arts of the Renaissance. The importance of the Venetian bead industry cannot be overestimated. At one time there were more than 250 separate bead-making firms; by the eighteenth century, the weekly output of the Venetian factories was more than twenty tons of finished beads. While the beauty of Venetian beads was unrivaled and their role in European fashion undiminished, it was their value as a trading currency in the newly discovered lands of the Americas, Africa, and Asia that fed the boom in production.

While glass beads were important within the East Indies trade, they played a much more central role in Africa and the New World. It is perhaps an apocryphal (if not untrue) story that the island of Manhattan was purchased for a few strands of glass beads, but it is undoubtedly true that vast quantities of merchandise and real estate were acquired in that way. Traders paid beads for furs in North America and for slaves in Africa. The extent of this reprehensible bead trade, facilitated by Venetian mass production, is reflected in the name given to the whole category of glass beads, African trading beads. These attractive beads were made not in Africa but in Venice; such was their value as a trading currency in Africa that they found a permanent home there for centuries. When modern bead collectors discovered these charms and started buying them as antiques, they kept the name of the beads' function rather than their origin. Today, the art of bead-weaving, in which tiny European seed beads are used to create a patterned "fabric" or to decorate a hide or cloth, is still practiced among both African and North American tribes.

The Venetians fought for centuries to keep their techniques secret, periodically imposing draconian penalties to prevent glassmakers from setting up shop elsewhere. But monopolies cannot last forever, and many other countries tried to develop their own glass bead industries. The most successful of these was a forested and mountainous region in northern Bohemia, which today is part of the Czech Republic. Endowed with plentiful quartz sand, as well as wood for fueling the furnaces and creating potash, Bohemia became a rival to Venice. By the end of the nineteenth century, Bohemia was leading the world in the production of glass beads for the fashion trade. The handsome art deco facades of the Bohemian "bead towns" attest to the early-twentieth-century boom in glass beads and the wealth created by the large-scale production of pressed glass, lampwork, and seed beads. The great crystal bead firms came out of this boom as well, though Swarovski, the most famous of these firms, sought an even more remote region of Europe to protect its trade secrets.

Later in the twentieth century, a large Japanese seed bead industry was developed, taking some of the market from the Czechs in much the same way the Czechs had taken it from the Venetians years earlier. Today, the Chinese are getting in on the global act, as the country's ancient traditions and skills in glass bead-making are increasingly exploited by the international marketplace. What is perhaps most exciting is the renaissance in lampwork beads by individual glass bead artists in the United States. Hundreds of fine American beadmakers, fueled by a love for the medium and without a tradition of their own, have kindled a renewed enthusiasm for glass bead design around the world. Yet, however the commercial production centers continue to change, and wherever artistic inspiration for the beads has been discovered, the ancient and universal appeal of these tiny glass objects remains constant.

TYPES OF GLASS USED FOR BEADS

SODA-LIME GLASS

This is the simplest and most common of glasses, forming most of our windows and light bulbs. It is composed primarily of sodium silicate, sodium carbonate, and calcium carbonate—a combination that has served glassmakers for several thousand years and is still widely used today.

BOROSILICATE GLASS

Very sudden changes in temperature can cause ordinary glass to shatter, an unfortunate event if it happens to hold the contents of your family's dinner or the results of a scientist's chemistry experiment. The challenge of making heat-resistant glass was overcome in Germany at the end of the nineteenth century by adding the mineral boron. As a result, chemistry labs are able to use test tubes and retorts without fear of destruction, and the glass pie dish has become one of the most common pieces of household cooking equipment. Although borosilicate glass needs a hotter flame to work, it also has some qualities that are attractive to lampwork beadmakers—it is crystal clear, difficult to break, and relatively easy to work with.

LEAD CRYSTAL

The art of making glass that was "crystal clear" long eluded large-scale producers. Then, in the thirteenth century, the Venetians combined pure quartz sand with ash from sea plants to create a glass of such clarity that they called it *cristallo*, after the clear rock crystal that it emulated. Others tried to imitate the Venetian product, but it was only surpassed in the seventeenth century when an Englishman named John Ravenscroft devised (with a little Venetian help) a commercial process to make a glass that was not only brilliantly clear but also easily cut to produce sharp, reflective surfaces. Part of the secret was the addition of a large amount of lead oxide, typically more than one quarter of the total compound. Today, lead crystal sets the standard for the highest quality crystal glass and is used to dazzling effect in beads.

DICHROIC GLASS

This is truly a high-tech glass that came out of space industry research and is dependent on the same physics that cause the rainbow effect in soap bubbles. Dichroic glass is made by vaporizing metallic salts in a vacuum so that they coat the surface of the glass. This produces a glass with a stunning iridescence, similar to that of the "fire" found in opals. Dichroic glass is expensive and difficult to work with, but when fused to certain kinds of other glass, it can be used to great effect in lampwork beads. Because the firing of dichroic glass changes its characteristics, each bead is original and unique.

LEAD GLASS

The addition of lead oxide to glass makes it softer, easier to work with at lower temperatures, and easier to cut and re-melt. Some lampwork and pressed beads use glass with a small amount of lead oxide.

GLASS BEAD VARIETIES

With few exceptions, the style, complexity, and cost of a glass bead is dependent on the method used to make it rather than on the glass itself. So important is this factor in the selection of glass beads that we use the production process as the first label in categorizing them. To know anything about glass beads, therefore, you have to know something about how they are made. The following is a description of the main types of glass bead production.

LAMPWORK

One of the earliest methods of bead-making was to melt a bit of glass and then wind it around a metal rod. Once the glass had cooled and hardened, you would take out the rod and be left with a round object with a hole in its middle—a bead. For obvious reasons, beads made in this way are referred to as wound glass. A more sophisticated version of wound glass was developed when beadmakers realized that if they kept the glass on the rod hot enough, they could add different colors of glass on top; all they needed was a flame directed toward the developing bead. At first the flame was supplied by an oil- or tallow-burning lamp, which gave the name *lampwork* to the beads produced in this way (they are also referred to as *flamework*). Since the flame of a lamp was not hot enough to melt the glass, beadmakers would blow air through a thin pipe and into the flame, increasing its heat and directing it toward the bead. A bellows was soon added to save the beadmakers' lungs although the ancient method of mouth blowing is still used in India.

Modern technology has replaced the old lamps with high-intensity torches that combine fuel and oxygen to focus high heat with pinpoint precision. Regardless of whether the heat source is a lamp or a torch, this type of bead-making provides the greatest scope of imagination, skill, and creativity both to the artist and to the artisan.

Since each bead is produced by hand, each is, to a degree, unique. The beadmaker starts with a selection of thin glass rods in different colors. Taking a long metal needle about the diameter of the hole of the bead, she or he melts the tip of a glass rod over a hot torch (the "lamp" or "flame") and catches the molten glass on the metal needle. As she or he twists the needle, the beadmaker can gather the molten glass in a ring around the needle. By keeping this core red-hot and melting other rods, she or he can add different colors and press or stretch the bead into whatever shape the design, or his or her imagination, calls for.

Because lampwork beads are the most labor-intensive to produce, they are generally the most expensive type of glass bead.

The production of lampwork beads is still a cottage industry in some parts of the world, with companies delivering glass rods to the homes of beadmakers and collecting their finished beads. The Czech Republic, Italy, Japan, India, and China all have important lampwork industries, but the most surprising development has been the renaissance of glass bead-making in the United States. Starting with just a handful of enthusiasts in the 1970s, American beadmakers now number in the thousands and include some of the most highly respected lampwork bead designers in the world.

DRAWN GLASS

Molten glass is amazingly elastic and can be stretched to great lengths without breaking. If you heat a blob of molten glass in a furnace, attach it to one end of a hollow metal tube, and give a good blow in the other end, the glass will expand like a balloon. Beadmakers have long used this quality to create the holes in beads. Simply puff to create a pocket of air, attach another rod to the other end of the red-hot balloon of glass, and start stretching. As the glass stretches out into a cylinder, the bubble of air is also stretched out, becoming smaller and smaller as the cylinder turns into a tube. Once the glass tube cools, it can be cut into small pieces; the trapped pocket becomes the hole of a bead. Since drawn glass can be stretched very evenly, all the little pieces cut from the tube look pretty much the same. And since it can be stretched very far—two to three hundred feet is not unusual—this method enables glassworkers to make hundreds or thousands of beads out of one batch of glass, a much easier process than to create them one by one over a hot flame.

Among the most commonly used products of this method of bead-making are seed beads. This is a generic term applied to very small glass beads produced in large quantities.

Any glass beads that are under four or five millimeters in diameter and do not have some obvious distinction (like the faceting of crystals) risk being lumped into this category. In modern processes the hot glass tube is not drawn by hand, but by gravity fed onto a conveyer or pulled by a wheel that draws it out at a constant speed. As the glass tube cools, it is cut into shorter lengths that are then chopped by a machine into tiny beads. These are then heated, tumbled, and polished to form rounded, smooth edges. The finished seed beads are either strung into hanks or sold by weight. Bugle beads are made the same way, except they are cut into longer lengths and their ends are not polished; so, you can see what a cane looks like before it is broken up into seed beads.

Glass canes are another product of the drawn glass method. Because molten glass stretches so evenly, any pattern or design it starts out with remains intact throughout the entire piece, simply getting smaller and smaller as the cane gets longer. By bundling together several layers or rods, beadmakers can easily create a design in a short, fat piece of glass and then stretch it out into a long, thin rod. When they cut the rod into little pieces, the end pattern of each piece will be exactly the same—a seemingly impossible, perfect miniature of the original. Venetian artisans were particularly famous for this kind of intricate glass work, even incorporating portraits of well-known people into their designs.

A contemporary example of the drawn glass method is a type of bead called furnace glass or art glass. While many glass beads start in a furnace, where the glass is melted, this expression has come to refer to a particular kind of modern drawn glass bead, one in which the core of the rod is coated with a clear glass. This kind of bead requires a large annealing kiln so that the bead can cool very slowly in order to avoid cracking.

BLOWN GLASS

Just as vases and bottles can be made by blowing air into a blob or, more elegantly expressed, a "gather" of molten glass, so, too, can beads be created by blowing glass on a small pipe to create a bubble-like shape. It is easier, however, to start with a thin-walled glass tube into which air can be blown by mouth or bellows. While individual and free-form beads can be made this way, larger-scale production is achieved through the use of heated glass tubes contained within a mold. One end of the tube is sealed. As air is blown into the other end, the sides of the tube expand to fill the bead-shaped areas of the mold. When the glass cools, there is a chain of glass bubbles that can be cut apart to make individual beads. This kind of bead was once popularly used to imitate pearls. After the bead chain was formed, a solution made of fish scales (called *essence d'orient*) was blown to coat the interior surface with a nacre-like sheen. The beads, filled with wax to make them appear solid, had a remarkably fine pearl-like appearance that could not wear off, as it was on the inside of the glass.

For the jewelry designer, one of the attractions of blown glass beads is that they can be both very large and very light. While they seem as if they should be too fragile for constant wear, they are surprisingly sturdy.

PRESSED GLASS

Pressed glass beads are produced in great number through a semi-mechanical process. First, a metal mold is created. The mold is in two halves. Each half has the shapes of a dozen or more beads side-by-side. The beadmaker uses thick glass rods, each about an inch in diameter. The beadmaker sits in front of a pressing machine with the glass rods sticking in a small furnace by his side. Once the end of a glass rod is the right temperature, the beadmaker lays it on the bottom half of the mold; the top half is then pressed down, forming the shape of the beads. At the same time, a set of metal

needles is thrust into holes in the side of the mold, piercing the glass to form the holes of the beads. The strip of beads comes out of the mold attached by a thin edge of glass. The beads are then broken off the strip, placed into a tumbling machine with sand or some other abrasive material, and tumbled for several hours to remove the edges and polish the glass to an even, smooth surface. With fire-polished beads, the rough pressed-glass beads are "polished" by being placed into a hot oven; the surface of the glass begins to melt and develops an attractive shine unique to this method.

COATED GLASS

Glass beads are often given distinction by the use of various surface coatings, on either the outside of the bead or the interior of the hole. The inventiveness of beadmakers has resulted in the creation of numerous methods, including glazing, etching, gilding, metalizing, staining, painting, iridizing, platinizing, and lustering—all of which can either subtly or completely change the characteristics of the original bead.

A popular coating is Aurora Borealis, or AB for short. As its name suggests, this coating adds a multihued iridescence to the surface.

Glass beads can also be metalized, or covered in metals, such as silver and gold. A particular style of seed bead called *silver-lined* gets its inner sparkle from having the hole lined with a metallic solution, giving it a silvery sheen.

CUT CRYSTAL

Like gemstones, glass can be faceted by cutting or grinding. Although this method is much more expensive than creating faceted pressed-glass beads, the difference is enormous. Even the best pressed and fire-polished glass beads lack the sharp edges and finely planed surface of cut glass. Because of its exceptional clarity and reflectivity, only crystal glass is used in this method. The best of these cut crystal beads, such as Swarovski, display a sparkle and brilliance that is a serious rival to the gemstones they often emulate. Cut crystal beads are prized for their precision and glitter and can be used to produce stunning jewelry. Sophisticated modern techniques are used to make them; consequently, their production methods are often cloaked in secrecy. More than a hundred years ago, the Swarovski family moved its production from the glass bead capital of Gablonz to the small village of Wattens, high in the Austrian Alps. There they found not only a source of hydro-electric power to operate their cutting machines but also a remote situation in which the confidentiality of their methods could be closely guarded.

PATÉ DE VERRE AND POWDERED GLASS

When glass is crushed and powdered, it can be mixed into a paste that can then be applied to a mold and fired to become fused and solid. While this method sounds very simple and can, if used casually, produce clumsy-looking beads, it can also, in the right hands, create beads of great intricacy and beauty. But it is a labor-intensive process and mainly practiced by individual artisans.

In Africa, colorful glass beads are made by crushing old glass into a powder and then mixing it into a paste with gum Arabic, which is then shaped and heated. The base core is then coated with more colored glass paste and heated again to form a patterned surface. Older beads made in this manner are often highly valued by collectors.

GLASS BEAD VARIETIES KEY
PAGE 16
1. Lampwork Opaque Glass
2. Various Lampwork Designs
3. Lampwork with Gold Foil
4. Charlottes
5. Pressed Glass with Seed Beads
6. Pressed and Coated Glass
7. Lampwork Dichroic Glass
8. Pressed Glass

PAGE 17
1. Chevron Beads (Venice)
2. American Lampwork (Nancy Pilgrim)
3. Millefiore (Venice)
4. Dichroic Glass (Luigi Catelan)
5. Bugle Beads
6. Bohemian Lampwork
7. Furnace Glass (Art Glass)
8. American Dichroic (Nikki Blanchard)
9. Glass Crystal
10. Seed Beads
11. Lampwork with Silver Foil (Bohemian)
12. Millefiore (Venice)
13. Pressed Glass
14. Blown Glass
15. Lampwork with Gold Foil

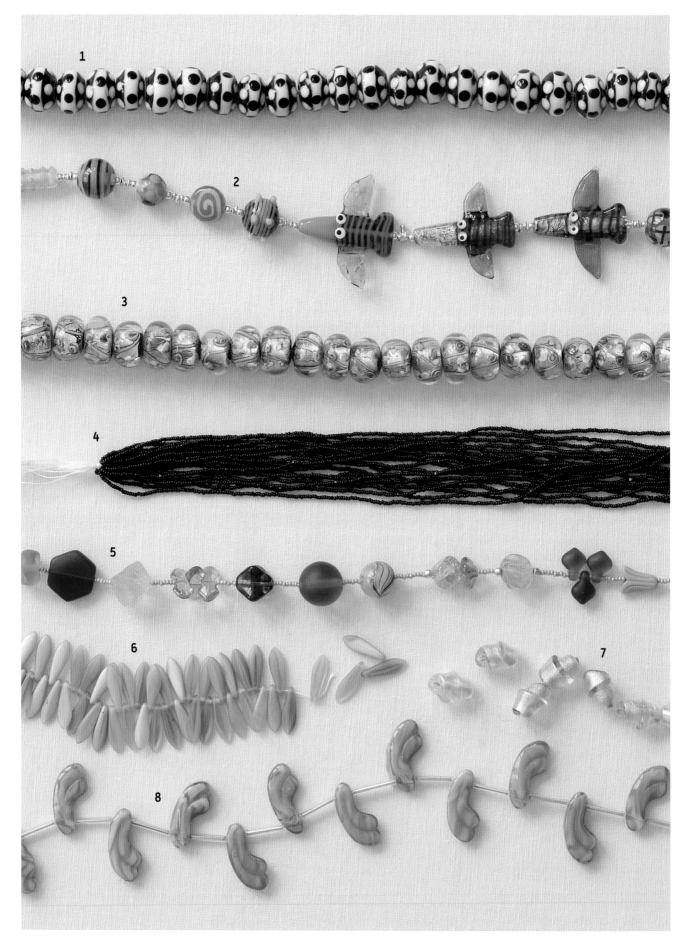

JEWELRY MAKING SUPPLIES

Before you rush out to buy any of the items below, read carefully through the list of materials and the tools needed to make a particular design. In recent years there has been a proliferation of bead stores around the world, making it easy and pleasant to acquire materials for making jewelry. If you do not have a local bead store, there are many mail order suppliers, most of whom have online stores.

TOOLS

It's surprising how few tools you need to make jewelry. For many necklaces and earrings, you can get away with just two: a pair of flat-nosed pliers and wire cutters. The other tools you need to make the designs in this book are detailed in Toolbox Essentials (right).

Some of these items you can find around the house, but you'll want to make a modest investment in tools specifically designed for jewelry makers, since they will make your life easier and your finished jewelry sturdy and long-lasting.

There are other specialist items that you can add as you go along, but the items above are all you really need. Some people like to lay out their necklaces on a bead design board, which has curved channels especially designed to hold your beads. For myself, I prefer to design sitting cross-legged on a comfortable carpet with all my beads and tools spread out around me. If you do design on a table or at a desk, you'll need something to stop the beads from rolling all over the place, either a bead mat or a thick, soft fabric like a towel.

TOOLBOX ESSENTIALS:

- A pair of wire cutters
- A pair of narrow flat-nosed pliers (also known as chain-nosed pliers)
- A pair of round-nosed pliers
- An awl
- A pair of crimping pliers (only for designs that are strung on beading wire)
- Scissors
- Beading needle (twisted wire)
- Hypo-cement glue (or clear nail polish)

STRINGING MATERIAL

The main structure of a neck-"lace" is, by definition, a piece of thin material that can be wrapped like a lace around the neck. This could be silk thread, leather thong, wire, chain, or one of the modern bead-stringing wires. Whatever the material, it must combine both strength and flexibility. Here are the materials recommended for the patterns in this book:

SILK

This is the traditional material for threading pearls, but it can be used to string any type of bead. It is reasonably strong, easy to work with, and very, very supple. While modern beading wire is stronger and easier to use, no other material allows a strand of beads to embrace the neck in quite the same way as silk. Although it is quite easy to thread beads onto silk by using a twisted wire beading needle, some makers now provide lengths of silk thread with a stiffened end that acts as its own eedle and can simply be cut off when you are finished with it.

Silk also has some distinct disadvantages: it will break when roughly handled, it will stretch over time, and it gets dirty which requires restringing. A good rule of thumb is that necklaces that are worn regularly should be restrung every one or two years.

Silk comes in several thicknesses, which are expressed by an arcane alphabetical code. The thickest silk thread is size FFF, while the thinnest is size 00. For these projects, we are going to use size F and keep things simple.

BEADING WIRE

Modern technology has tried to overcome the disadvantages of silk while retaining its qualities of flexibility and ease of use. This was a surprisingly difficult task, and the only material to come close is a relatively new and sophisticated product. Beading wires seem simple— just a few twisted strands of wire coated in plastic. But early attempts were frustratingly inadequate. The wire was too stiff to lie around the neck gracefully; it would kink if bent sharply, and it would break if mishandled. Today's 19- and 49-strand beading wires are increasingly kink-resistant; they don't break under normal use and, although still not quite as supple as silk, they are very flexible. With the logic of an industry more used to hardware than jewelry, the manufacturers of beading wire have decided to measure its thickness in inches. This completely ignores the fact that the holes in beads \are measured in millimeters. So to keep things simple again, we recommend using just one kind of beading wire for most designs, the best quality 49-strand size .015.

CHAIN

Whatever style of chain you prefer, I recommend that you use sterling silver and gold-filled chain for any jewelry you intend to wear for a long time. Plated chain is much more inexpensive and it has an appropriate place for fashion items that you do not expect to be long-lived—its plating will eventually wear away, leaving unattractive base metal. Solid gold chain is, of course, nice to have, but very expensive. In appearance and durability, gold-filled chain is the next best thing.

WIRE

Stringing beads together with wire is easier than it first appears. In these designs we use just two types: sterling silver and gold-filled, both in a "half-hard" density. Wire is sold in another traditional measurement, "gauge." The wire used for the designs in this book is 20 gauge, corresponding to .032 of an inch.

SPACERS

Spacers are just beads that create spaces between other larger or more important beads. Theoretically, any beads could act as spacers, but in practice, they tend to be fairly simple silver and gold beads, although they are sometimes more elaborate. For some designs, glass and glass crystal beads are used as spacers. Their most important characteristic is that they should emphasize and not overwhelm the main beads.

The most versatile of all spacers, gold and silver rounds, can be used wherever a bigger bead needs to be emphasized, or at the beginning and end of strands to cover up beading wire and give a nice visual "tailing off" effect. If they are over 2.5mm in size, I recommend you use seamless hollow sterling silver and seamless hollow gold-filled spacers.

DAISIES

Painstakingly constructed using a method called *granulation*, these are little silver or gold disks onto which tiny drops of the same metal have been applied around the edge. Used singly or in a group, they have a rich reflective texture that is delightful to the eye and to the touch.

CHARLOTTES AND OTHER SEED BEADS

Often the best choice for use between small- or medium-sized beads, these tiny glass beads come in a large range of colors. When charlottes are gold- or silver-plated, they can be amazingly beautiful and provide a glittering string of light between the principal beads.

RONDELS

Like little donuts, these beads are made for embracing the sides of larger round beads. When set in between two larger rounds, rondels make a pleasing little band that gives a certain solidity to the design. Glass rondels are a great way to add color to a plain design.

FINDINGS

These linking pieces are the essential hardware of the jewelry maker. Just as the toolkit of a carpenter is filled with nails, screws, and bolts to construct his works, the jeweler has her stock of clasps, wires, and links. There are many hundreds of different findings available, but you need only a few to make the jewelry in *A Touch of Glass*. Most findings come in different metals, and you should always use the one that is appropriate to the design.

FINDINGS FOR NECKLACES
BEAD TIPS

This finding is for attaching the end of a necklace thread to the clasp. It is designed to grip on to the knot you make after the last bead and comes in two varieties, the basket bead tip and the clamshell. The former works by trapping the knot in a little "basket" while the latter sandwiches it between two concave wings that look like clamshells.

CRIMPS

Crimps are tiny metal beads that can be crushed flat with pliers. When beading wire is threaded through a bead crimp, through the loop of a clasp, and then back through the crimp, all you need to do is firmly, but carefully, squash the little crimp to attach the wire to the clasp. So easy and useful are these little clamps that there is even a specialist tool, crimping pliers, that helps exert the right amount of pressure for a perfect seal. But you can also close them with simple flat-nosed pliers. Leather and cord crimps are even easier to use; just slip them over the end of the cord, and squeeze them to create a finished end.

CLASPS

Unless you are making a necklace big enough to fit over your head, you will need some kind of a clasp to finish it off. Clasps for necklaces and bracelets come in a staggering variety of styles and use several different methods to attach their two halves, but they all fall into a few basic categories and are all attached to the necklace in pretty much the same way.

CRIMP COVERS

These provide an easy way of disguising the messy part of the necklace between the clasp and the first and last beads. They are hollow spheres that open up like clamshells. You simply fit them over the flattened crimp and gently squeeze them shut. Once in place, they look just like a smooth round silver or gold bead. Although these findings are not necessary to make a necklace, they can add an extra touch of sophistication to your designs.

THE BASIC MATERIALS IN DESCENDING ORDER OF COST AND/OR QUALITY ARE:

GOLD Use only with high-value beads.

GOLD-FILLED Use with any good-quality beads.

VERMEIL (sterling silver plated with gold) Use with good-quality beads.

NIOBIUM (hypo-allergenic metal) Use if you have an allergic reaction to silver.

SILVER (sterling or better) Use with good quality beads.

PLATED BASE METAL OR PLASTIC Use on less expensive jewelry that is not expected to last. (There are some very fine plate metals and plastics that are exceptions to this rule.)

FINDINGS FOR EARRINGS
EARWIRES
These are the bits that actually attach to your ear. If you have pierced ears, use earwires designed to fit through the pierced hole. If your ears are not pierced or if you feel like a change, use ones that clamp onto your ear with a clip or a screw. Earwires worn through your ear should always be of good quality and composed of a material like sterling silver that will not cause an allergic reaction.

FINDINGS COMMON TO BOTH NECKLACES AND EARRINGS
HEADPINS AND EYEPINS
These are simple pieces of straight wire on which you thread your beads. The "head" or "eye" at one end prevents the beads from falling off, and the other end is attached to the earwire.

JUMP RINGS, SPLIT RINGS, AND PLAIN RINGS
These rings are often used for linking parts of necklaces and earrings. They all perform the same job but in slightly different ways. A jump ring is just a simple metal loop that can be opened and closed by twisting. A split ring cannot be opened, but the item to be connected can be slipped on to it by feeding it around the split in the side of the ring. Split rings are just miniature versions of the metal rings you probably use to hold your keys. A plain ring is one that cannot be opened as the ends are soldered together.

FINDINGS KEY
PAGE 22
1. Gold-Filled Shepherd's Hook Earwire (Left) "Add-On" Earwire (Right)
2. Silver and Gold-Filled Crimp Beads
3. Silver Bead Caps
4. Silver Leverback Earwire (Left) Earwire with Ball (Right)
5. Silver Bead Caps
6. Silver and Gold-Filled Crimp Covers
7. Antiqued Silver Bead Caps
8. Silver And Gold-Filled Basket Bead Tips
9. Vermeil Headpins With Ball Tip
10. Gold-Filled Headpins
11. Silver and Gold-Filled Eyepin
12. Silver and Gold-Filled Rings
13. Silver Jump Rings
14. Silver and Vermeil Headpins With Ball Tip

PAGE 23
15. Gold-Filled Lobster Clasp
16. Silver And Marcasite Toggle Clasp
17. Vermeil Lobster Clasp
18. Silver Box Clasp
19. Silver and Marcasite Toggle Clasp
20. Gold-Filled Box Clasp
21. Gold-Filled Box Clasp
22. Gold-Filled Lobster Clasp
23. Vermeil Toggle Clasp
24. "Stardust" Silver Toggle Clasp
25. Vermeil Lobster Clasp
26. Silver Hook and Eye Clasp
27. Silver Toggle Clasp
28. Vermeil Toggle Clasp
29. Silver Hook and Eye Clasp
30. Gold-Filled Three-Strand Sliding Clasp
31. Silver Hook and Eye Clasp
32. Gold-Filled Spring Ring Clasp
33. Silver Toggle Clasp

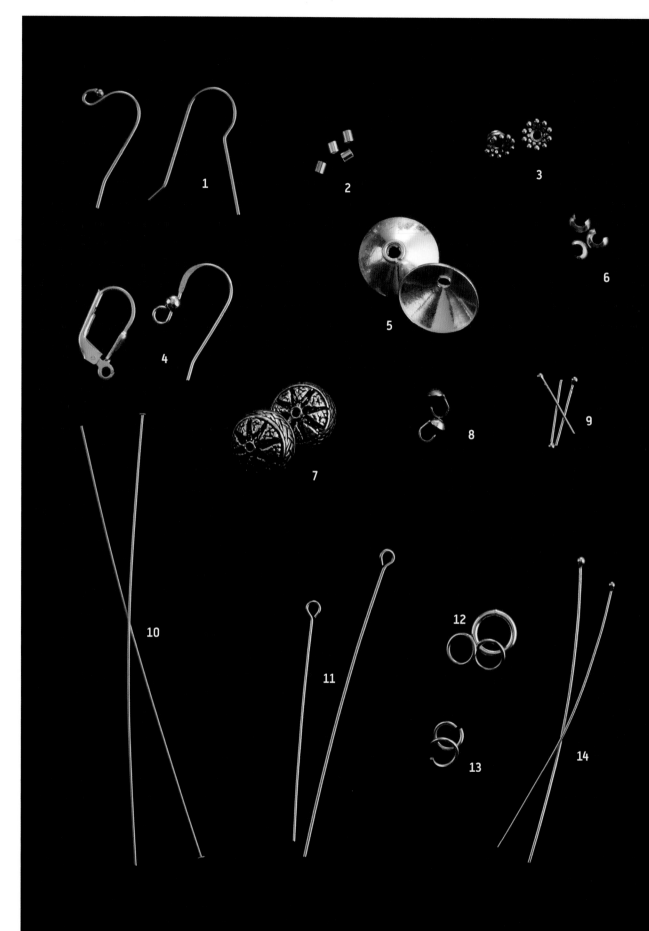

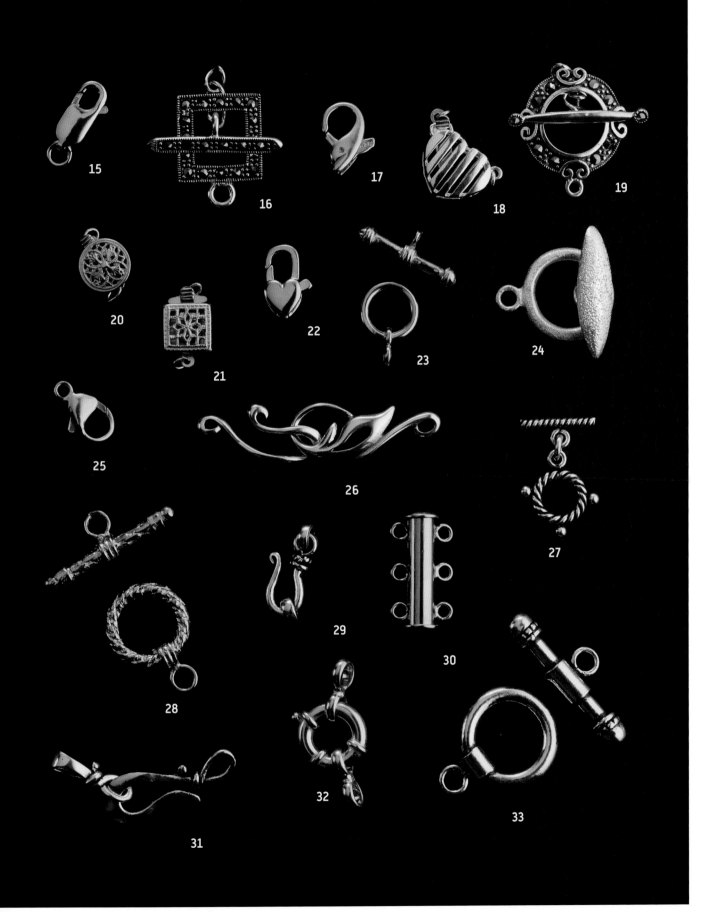

15

16

17

18

19

20

21

22

23

24

25

26

27

28

29

30

31

32

33

JUST GLASS

MAKING JEWELRY
WITH GLASS BEADS

Making necklaces and earrings is simplicity itself. Although you still have to turn to the professional jeweler for setting rings and casting metals, you can master the basic techniques of stringing beads and bending wire in an evening. Combine these simple skills with a few inexpensive tools, add the basic ingredients of beads and findings, and you are ready to start making your own jewelry. Don't be intimidated! Compared to producing a decent meal, making a piece of jewelry is child's play—it requires fewer tools, and there are no dishes to wash up!

Every necklace or pair of earrings begins with the design. While it is perfectly possible to throw random beads on a string, the results are very unlikely to bring satisfaction.

My own view of jewelry design begins with a simple premise: "The purpose of any body decoration is to enhance the look of the wearer." I care, therefore, that the design will go well with the wearer's face, her clothes, her mood, and the impression she wishes to make. Some designers might take the approach that the body is just a convenient frame to exhibit an interesting object. If you are making jewelry for yourself, however, I have little doubt you will be more sympathetic to the view that the jewels are there to make you look good, not the other way round. While the jewelry in this book is in every way contemporary, it uses classic styles and materials that consistently return to the forefront of fashion and have a proven record of making their owners feel they are wearing the "right stuff."

Although you can follow the design instructions to simply replicate the jewelry in this book, do not be reluctant to try variation. A particular characteristic of glass beads is that an individual style will often come in several colors. Indeed, some styles of glass beads such as crystals and seed beads come in dozens or hundreds of different hues. Only in a few cases have I actually specified a particular color in the materials list. You can always use the same colors as those in the illustrations, but you should think of the instructions more like cooking recipes, where even small changes of ingredients can create a different but delightfully unique flavor.

Whether through desire for experimentation or a simple lack of access to the precise "ingredients," you should not be afraid of substitution to create your own unique "dish." Making these designs will, after all, be even more rewarding if they include a dash of your own good design judgment.

It is my hope that, after you have made a few of the designs in this book, you will use your skills and your own design sense to purposely introduce variation and then to starting creating entirely new designs of your own.

Whether substituting ingredients or planning a whole new design, you should follow these basic guidelines:

1. Do not mix inappropriate materials. While it is obvious that you would not use plastic beads with rubies or real pearls with wood beads, the rule can quickly enter the gray area of subjective opinion. In case you are not yet ready to trust your own eye, Chapter 3, "Touches of Glass" includes suggestions for some of the materials that do match well.

2. No matter what they actually cost, never use materials that look cheap. They will simply make the good look bad.

3. Use materials that have a fashion lifespan of decades rather than weeks. Today's fad is tomorrow's toast.

Before you attempt any of the projects in this book, you will need to read the instructions for basic jewelry making in Chapter 4, "Jewelry Techniques." This chapter includes information on stringing, making continuous strands, attaching clasps, wrapping wire, measuring, and using essential tools. Read Chapter 4 carefully, but note that these techniques are best learned through actual practice. When you feel comfortable, jump in and get started. As with all crafts, the only way to master the art of jewelry making is by actually doing it.

DESIGNING FOR YOU

When you are making jewelry for yourself or for friends or family, you have the opportunity to create something custom-built. Try matching the colors with favorite clothes, to skin and hair tones, or to an inherent preference for one shade or another. But you should also consider size. Bigger necks and busts obviously call for longer necklaces, but the size of the actual beads can be just as important. In designing commissioned pieces, my first thoughts are always to the shape of the client—the more delicate the bone structure and more petite her size, the more delicate the jewelry.

While fashion and mood will dictate overall bead sizes, the general rule, "bigger women need bigger beads," is usually proved right. Size in jewelry is as important as size in clothing. No piece should either overwhelm, or be overwhelmed by, the body that wears it. In jewelry design, the goal is harmony, not competition.

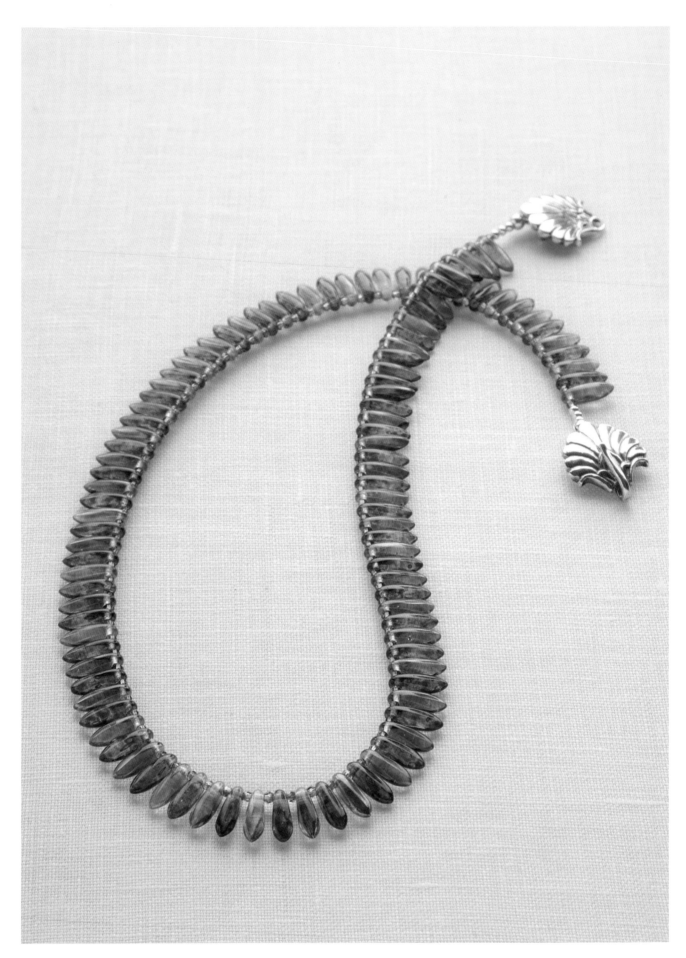

PRESSED GLASS AND CRYSTAL NECKLACE

ALTHOUGH PRESSED GLASS BEADS ARE MORE ECONOMICAL THAN LAMPWORK BEADS, THEY CAN NONETHELESS BE USED TO CREATE EQUALLY ELEGANT AND SOPHISTICATED JEWELRY. THIS NECKLACE RELIES ON TWO COMPLEMENTARY TONES FOR ITS EFFECT——ONE, A SIMPLE BUT PLEASANT BLUE; THE OTHER, A LIGHT GREEN WITH A MOTTLED AMBER COATING KNOWN AS A PICASSO FINISH. THE LITTLE "DAGGER" SHAPES REQUIRE SPACER BEADS BETWEEN EACH TO ENSURE THEY HANG PROPERLY. USING A TINY AMBER CRYSTAL BEAD ADDS A DASH OF SPARKLE AT THE BASE OF THE MAIN GLASS BEADS WHILE SERVING AS A SPACER. USING SILVER BEADING WIRE ADDS REFLECTIVITY TO THE TRANSPARENT CRYSTAL BEADS FOR EXTRA SHINE AND INTEREST.

1. Start the necklace by threading on a crimp. Pass the beading wire through the ring of one half of the clasp and then back through the crimp. Make sure that the beading wire is tight around the ring. Squeeze the crimp shut with crimping pliers.

2. Thread on three 2mm silver beads.

3. Now add a crystal bead, a blue pressed glass bead, another crystal bead, and then a mottled green pressed glass bead. Repeat this pattern fifty-two times; then, add the final blue pressed glass bead.

4. Check the necklace around your neck to make sure that it is the right length. Add three 2mm silver beads and one crimp. Bring the beading wire through the ring of the other side of the clasp and then back through the crimp and round bead. Now, tighten the necklace so there are no spaces between the beads, close the crimp, and snip off any remaining beading wire. Add the crimp covers.

TOOLS
Wire Cutters, Crimping Pliers

MATERIALS

107	3mm x 10mm pressed glass top-drilled dagger shaped beads in two colors—53 mottled green and 54 blue
108	2mm round Swarovski crystal beads
6	2mm silver hollow seamless round beads
1	sterling silver hook and eye clasp
2	silver crimp beads
2	silver crimp bead covers
20"	of silver beading wire

SILVER CHAIN AND LAMPWORK NECKLACE

THESE BEAUTIFUL GLASS BEADS ARE DESIGNED AND MADE BY CZECH ARTIST ALENA CHLADKOVA. TRANSPARENT BANDS OF GLASS ARE LAID AS RIDGES ON THE CENTRAL CORE, GIVING TEXTURE AND INTERESTING LIGHT EFFECTS TO THE BEADS. THIS NECKLACE IS A CLASSIC EXAMPLE OF HOW FINE DESIGN AND THE INDIVIDUAL MERIT OF EACH HAND-CRAFTED BEAD CALL FOR A SETTING OF SOLID SILVER.

1. Start by attaching each of the glass beads to a piece of looped wire in the following manner: Using your round-nosed pliers, make a simple loop at one end of the silver wire. Thread a silver bead onto the wire; then, add a glass bead and another silver bead. Make sure they are snug against one another and against the loop; then, cut the wire about $1/4$" above the last bead. Make a simple loop, ensuring that the bottom of the loop fits snugly against the round bead. Repeat this process for the rest of the silver and glass beads.

2. Cut the chain into twenty-two pieces, each three links long. (Tip: For each piece, you will have one unused link. Save all these cut links, along with any other scraps of silver wire your work generates. When you have collected enough of this "waste," you can take it to a smelter and collect on the value of the silver.)

3. Arrange your glass beads in a pleasing manner. The pattern I have used is as follows: barrel, 12mm round, rectangle, 10mm round, 12mm round, B, 10mm, R, B, 12mm, 10mm, R, B, 12mm, R, 10mm, B, 12mm, B, R, 12mm, 10mm. Attach a glass bead to the end of a piece of chain by opening the loop, slipping it on the end link of the piece of chain, and then closing it. Attach the next glass bead to the other end of the chain. Continue adding beads and chain lengths until you have used them all. To complete the loop, attach the end link of the chain to the other side of the glass bead you started with.

TOOLS
Wire Cutters, Round-Nosed Pliers, Flat-Nosed Pliers

MATERIALS (TO MAKE A 28" ROPE LENGTH)
5	10mm round lampwork glass beads
6	12mm round lampwork glass beads
5	14mm x 16mm flat rectangular lampwork glass beads (R)
6	16mm x 9mm barrel lampwork glass beads (B)
44	2.5mm seamless hollow silver beads
12"	silver chain with 5mm oval links
30"	20 gauge silver wire

TIP: WORKING THE WIRE THIS WAY IS FAR LESS WASTEFUL THAN CUTTING PRESET LENGTHS OF WIRE. BECAUSE THE BEADS ARE DIFFERENT SIZES, THEY WILL USE DIFFERENT LENGTHS OF WIRE. IF YOU CUT EACH PIECE FROM THE WHOLE LENGTH OF WIRE AS YOU MAKE IT, YOU WILL HAVE ALMOST NO WASTE AT THE END.

LEOPARD BEAD NECKLACE

THESE BEAUTIFUL GREEN LAMPWORK BEADS ARE MADE IN THE CZECH REPUBLIC BY ALEALE. THEIR MARVELOUS INNER REFLECTION IS CREATED WITH REAL GOLD FOIL WRAPPED AROUND THE CENTRAL CORE OF EACH BEAD. THE DESIGN OF THESE BEADS IS BEAUTIFULLY ACCENTED BY COMPLEMENTARY GOLD BEADS. THIS PARTICULAR PIECE FEATURES IMPRESSIVE GLASS BEADS THAT RIVAL—IF NOT SURPASS—THE BEAUTY AND EXPENSE OF MANY GEMSTONES. BOTH THEIR COLOR AND THEIR VALUE ARE APPROPRIATELY MATCHED WITH GOLD-FILLED BEAD CAPS AND SPACER BEADS.

1. Thread a crimp onto the beading wire. Pass the beading wire through the ring of the one half of the clasp and then back through the crimp. Make sure that the beading wire is tight around the ring. Squeeze the crimp shut. Thread on a gold bead, a 2.5mm bead, two 3mm beads, and another 2.5mm bead.

2. Add a bead cap (convex side facing the gold beads), a glass bead, another bead cap (concave side facing the glass bead), and a 2.5mm bead. Repeat this pattern thirty-two times.

3. Try the necklace on for size. Add two 3mm beads and a 2.5mm bead. Add a crimp. Bring the beading wire through the ring of the other side of the clasp and then back through the crimp and the round bead. Now, tighten the necklace so there are no spaces between the beads, close the crimp, and snip off any remaining beading wire. Add the crimp covers.

TOOLS

Wire Cutters, Crimping Pliers

MATERIALS

- 33 17mm disc-shaped lampwork glass beads with gold foil interiors
- 66 4.5mm gold-filled beads caps
- 4 3mm gold-filled hollow seamless round beads
- 17 2.5mm gold-filled hollow seamless round beads
- 1 16mm vermeil toggle clasp
- 2 gold-filled crimp beads
- 2 gold-filled bead covers
- 20" of gold colored beading wire

FLOWER BEADS NECKLACE

THE ART OF MAKING GLASS BEADS WITH MANY LITTLE GLASS FLOWERS INSIDE HAS LONG BEEN A HALLMARK OF BOHEMIAN BEAD MAKERS. THE CZECHS, HOWEVER, HAVE STUCK TO BEADS WITH JUST TWO OR THREE SETS OF FLOWERS. THESE BEADS ARE FROM CHINA, WHERE BEADMAKERS HAVE LEARNED THE BOHEMIAN TECHNIQUE AND EXPANDED IT BY FILLING THE ENTIRE BEAD WITH FLOWERS. IT IS EASY TO APPRECIATE THE TIME AND SKILL INVESTED IN EACH ONE OF THESE BEADS. ALTHOUGH THEY ARE NOT EXPENSIVE, THEIR VALUE AS FINE ARTISTIC WORK LEAD ME TO USE CYLINDRICAL VERMEIL SPACERS BETWEEN EACH ONE.

1. Thread a crimp onto the beading wire. Pass the beading wire through the ring of one half of the clasp and then back through the crimp. Make sure that the beading wire is tight around the ring. Squeeze the crimp shut. Thread on a 3mm gold-filled bead, a 4mm bead, and another 3mm bead.

2. Add a glass bead, a 3mm bead, a vermeil cylinder, and another 3mm bead. Repeat this pattern twenty-one times.

3. Add a 3mm, a 4mm, and a 3mm bead. Bring the beading wire through the ring of the other side of the clasp and back through the crimp and round bead. Now tighten the necklace so there are no spaces between the beads, close the crimp, and snip off any remaining beading wire. Add the crimp covers.

4. Make the dangle by adding a 3mm bead, a glass bead, a 3mm bead, a vermeil cylinder, and another 3mm bead to the headpin. Make the beginnings of a wire-wrapped loop (page 135). Hook it over one end of the necklace wire between the crimp cover and the first bead. Finish attaching by wire wrapping the loop. Snip off any excess wire.

TOOLS
Wire Cutters, Crimping Pliers

MATERIALS
- 23 12mm glass flower beads
- 22 5.5mm vermeil side-drilled decorated cylinders
- 49 3mm gold-filled hollow seamless round beads
- 2 4mm gold-filled hollow seamless round beads
- 1 2" gold-filled headpin with ball tip
- 1 12mm vermeil bolt ring clasp
- 2 gold-filled crimp beads
- 2 gold-filled bead covers
- 28" of gold color beading wire

GRADUATED DICHROIC GLASS CHOKER

ONE USUALLY THINKS OF ROUND BEADS WHEN DESIGNING
GRADUATED NECKLACES, BUT IRREGULAR SHAPES CAN ALSO
WORK WELL. ONE THEORY BEHIND THE APPEAL OF GRADUATED
NECKLACES, ESPECIALLY IN THE CASE OF PEARLS AND OTHER
GEMS, IS THAT THE SMALLER, CHEAPER BEADS ARE BEHIND
THE NECK, OFTEN UNDER YOUR HAIR, AND THUS NOT AS
VISIBLE. GRADUATED NECKLACES ARE NOT JUST FOR ECONOMY,
HOWEVER; THEY HAVE A VISUAL APPEAL OF THEIR OWN,
INCREASING THE SENSE OF PERSPECTIVE AND DRAWING
THE EYE ALONG THE NECK.

1. Start by arranging your dichroic beads on a bead board or soft
   fabric surface. Put the largest bead in the center and the next
   two largest beads on either side. Continue adding pairs of
   slightly smaller beads on either side of the central ones until
   you have used all the beads. Now, check the arrangement to
   make sure the color pattern is pleasing and the graduated
   effect is apparent.

2. Thread a crimp onto the beading wire. Pass the wire through
   the ring of one half of the clasp and then back through the
   crimp. Make sure that the beading wire is tight around the
   ring. Squeeze the crimp shut. Add two 3mm gold round beads
   to cover the tail of the beading wire and cut away any visible
   excess wire.

3. Thread on a 4mm gold bead and the first of your dichroic beads.
   Continue in this manner until you have used all the dichroic
   beads. Try the necklace to check the pattern and length.

4. Add a 4mm gold bead, two 3mm beads, and a crimp. Bring the
   beading wire through the ring of the other side of the clasp and
   then back through the crimp and one or two of the round beads.
   Now, tighten the necklace so there are no spaces between the
   beads, close the crimp, and snip off any remaining beading wire.
   Add the crimp covers.

TOOLS
Wire Cutters, Crimping Pliers

MATERIALS

21	13mm dichroic glass beads from 9mm to 18mm in size
22	4mm gold-filled hollow seamless faceted round beads
4	3mm gold-filled hollow seamless round beads
2	gold-filled crimp beads
2	gold-filled crimp covers
1	vermeil toggle clasp
22"	of beading wire

"END OF DAY" CHOKER

THE ROMANTIC NAME FOR THESE LOVELY VENETIAN BEADS HAS A RATHER PEDESTRIAN ORIGIN. AT THE END OF EACH DAY IN A BEAD-MAKING WORKSHOP, ALL THE LEFTOVER SCRAPS OF GLASS WOULD BE SAVED AND THEN MELTED TOGETHER WITH CLEAR GLASS TO FORM COLORFUL BEADS WITH RANDOM PATTERNS THAT LOOK LIKE LITTLE JACKSON POLLACK PAINTINGS. TO MAKE THE CHOKER AS FLEXIBLE AS POSSIBLE AROUND THE NECK, I HAVE USED SILK THREAD AS THE STRINGING MATERIAL. SINCE NO SINGLE COLOR THREAD WOULD MATCH THE SWIRLS OF STRONG COLORS IN THE BEADS, I USED THREE DIFFERENT COLORED THREADS TOGETHER; THIS PRODUCES LARGE KNOTS BETTER SUITED TO SUCH LARGE BEADS. I HAVE USED A LARGE BALL-SHAPED SCREW-CLASP TO MATCH THE SIZE AND SHAPE OF THE "END OF DAY" BEADS.

1. If you have never strung on silk before, read the section about knotting with silk (page 128) and practice the technique before starting. Once you are familiar with this technique, begin your necklace by grouping the three strands of silk together. Pass them through the eye of the twisted wire needle until they are doubled; then, tie a knot at the end.

2. Use the instructions in the how-to section (page 130) to attach a bead tip to the end of the thread. Then, add an "End of Day" bead and make a knot. Repeat this until you have used all your beads or until the length around your neck is as long as you want it.

3. Add the bead tip to the other end of the thread and attach both bead tips to the clasp.

TOOLS

Awl, Flat-Nosed Pliers, Twisted Wire Needle, Hypo cement or Clear Nail Polish

MATERIALS (TO MAKE A 15" CHOKER)

23 18mm Venetian "End of Day" beads

1 16mm Italian silver-plated screw clasp

2 large silver clamshell bead tips

60" of red size F silk thread

60" of blue size F silk thread

60" of yellow size F silk thread

SEED BEAD THREE-STRAND NECKLACE

SINCE SEED BEADS ARE VERY SMALL, IT IS COMMON TO
INCORPORATE MULTIPLE STRANDS INTO A PIECE TO CREATE
A BIGGER IMPRESSION. THE ELEGANT SILVER CONE AT THE
END OF THIS NECKLACE GIVES THE SEED BEADS A MORE
SOPHISTICATED LOOK. THE BEADS SPILL OUT FROM THE
SILVER LIKE A SMALL CORNUCOPIA.

1. Cut the silver wire into two 3" pieces. Make a wire-wrapped loop
   (page 135) at one end of each piece. Wrap several times around
   the base of each loop—the loops need to be strong enough to
   hold the three strands of beads.

2. Thread a crimp onto the beading wire. Pass it through one
   of the loops you just made and then back through the crimp.
   Tighten the beading wire on the loop and squeeze the crimp
   shut, cutting away any excess beading wire. Now thread on
   fifteen seed beads.

3. Add a rondel and seven seed beads. Repeat this pattern thirty-
   seven times; then, add another fifteen seed beads and a crimp.
   Pass the wire through the loop of the other piece of silver wire
   and then back through the crimp. Make sure all of the beads are
   tight against one another. Close the crimp. Cut away the balance
   of the wire.

4. Make the second strand exactly the same way as the first, but
   start and finish with only thirteen seed beads.

5. Make the third strand exactly the same way as the first, but start
   and finish with only eleven seed beads.

6. Pass the unlooped end of one of the pieces of silver wire
   through the wide end of a cone and out through the hole at
   the narrow end. Add a 3mm silver bead to the wire, and make a
   simple loop (page 135). Open the loop and attach it to one half
   of the clasp. Repeat the procedure to attach the other end of the
   necklace to the clasp.

TOOLS
Wire Cutters, Crimping Pliers

MATERIALS (FOR A 21" NECKLACE)
(about) 900 size 11/0 seed beads

117	4mm faceted glass rondels
2	44mm x 6mm silver curved cones
2	3mm silver hollow seamless round beads
1	10mm silver toggle clasp
6	silver crimp beads
6"	of 20 gauge silver wire
66"	of beading wire

PRESSED GLASS WITH LAMPWORK CENTERPIECE LARIAT

WHEN YOU WANT TO HIGHLIGHT A UNIQUE PIECE OF LAMPWORK GLASS, LESS EXPENSIVE PRESSED GLASS CAN OFTEN PLAY A SUPPORTING ROLE. THE LARGE LAMPWORK BEAD AT THE END OF THIS LARIAT IS BY AMERICAN GLASS ARTIST KEVIN O'GRADY, WHO CREATES LIMITED-EDITION JEWEL-LIKE BEADS. ALTHOUGH THE PRESSED GLASS FORMS MOST OF THE LENGTH OF THE LARIAT, I ADDED SILVER BEADS AND PEARLS TO ENSURE THAT THE VALUE OF THE CENTRAL BEAD IS NOT UNDERSTATED.

1. Put the lampwork bead onto the bead nail or add the silver disc and the lampwork bead to a silver headpin; make a wrapped loop. Add a crimp to the beading wire. Pass it through the hole in the bead nail or wrapped loop and then back through the crimp. Close the crimp.

2. Add the beads in a random pattern. If you wish to copy my pattern exactly, the sequence is B, B, 3E, A, E, C, 3E, B, A, E, B, E, A, D, A, D, A, E, H, E, H, E, H, E, H, flat oval bead, L, A, B0, F, 3E, F, L, J, H, G, 2E, A, H, J, 3E, B, 3E, J, B, F, 3E, A, D, A, D, A, E, H, E, H, E, L, G, L, H, J, H, 5E, B, 3E, L, G, H, 3E, H, J, H, 3E, B, 3E, L, H, G, H, L, 3E, A, H, J, H, L, 5E, B, E, G, H, L, 3E, J, D, A, E, H, E, L, A, H, glass bead cap, 2E.

3. Now, add a bead crimp. Continue adding the following: E, L, 2E, H, 3E, L, K, L, K, L, 3E, L, K, L, 2E, L, H, 4E, L, K, L, E, H, 2E, L, K, L, E, L, E, L. Pass the wire back through the first seed bead of this sequence and through the crimp. Make sure the loop and all the other beads are snug on the wire; then, close the crimp and snip off any remaining tail of the beading wire. To wear, drop the lampwork bead through the loop.

TOOLS
Wire Cutters, Crimping Pliers

MATERIALS

1	large and impressive lampwork glass bead (bead pictured is 25mm x 17mm)
1	large "bead nail" or 2" silver headpin and 5mm silver disc bead
14	7mm round pressed glass beads (A)
12	assorted granulated silver Bali-style beads from 5mm to 9mm (B)
1	10mm x 8mm flat rectangle pressed glass bead (C)
5	9mm pressed glass rondel beads (D)
80	size 8/0 black seed beads (E)
1	21mm x 15mm flat oval pressed glass bead
1	10mm x 15mm pressed glass bead cap
3	4mm round pressed glass beads (F)
5	15mm x 9mm vintage pressed glass beads (G)
21	assorted silver daisy spacer beads ranging from 4mm to 6mm (H)
6	6mm peacock potato or round pearls (J)
5	4mm bicone Swarovski crystal beads (style 5301) (K)
20	2.5mm hollow round silver beads (L)
2	silver crimp beads
25"	of beading wire

CRYSTAL AND SEED BEAD LARIAT

THIS IS A GREAT WAY TO USE UP CRYSTAL BEADS LEFT OVER FROM OTHER PROJECTS. USE A FEW GOLD-PLATED AND AB-COATED CRYSTALS TO MATCH THE GOLD REFLECTION OF THE CHARLOTTES.

1. Cut the beading wire into two 54" pieces and three 26" pieces. To one of the long pieces, add three 2.5mm beads, the loop of the toggle ring, and three more 2.5mm beads on the cone so the beads and toggle loop are sitting inside of it. Now, pass the other long piece of beading wire through the same beads so its ends are even with the first strand. Place the tip of the cone in the center of the beading wire strands. Turn the ends of the wires on the round bead side of the cone into its base and through the tip. Adjust them so the ends of the doubled strands are even. You should now have a loop of round gold beads holding the toggle ring, which should fit neatly inside the cone, with four even lengths of beading wire stretching away from the tip of the cone.

2. Take the three shorter lengths of beading wire and fit their ends through a single large crimp bead. Squeeze the crimp very tight so it grips all three strands at their ends. Pass the free ends of the three strands through the inside of the cone and out the tip. Pull the free ends of the strands to work the crimped end down inside the cone until it is caught at the tip. Adjust the strands on the toggle ring loop, if necessary, so the crimp is hidden by the cone. All the strands should now be held securely inside the cone, with seven lengths of beading wire stretching away from the tip of the cone.

3. Add the charlotte beads, the smaller crystal beads, the daisy beads, and the round gold beads to one of the lengths of beading wire. This pattern is random, but you can use the illustration for reference. When you have beaded between 22" and 24" of the strand or have at least 2" still bare, add one crimp bead and one of the larger crystal beads. Now, add a single charlotte bead and turn the beading wire back through

TOOLS
Wire Cutters, Crimping Pliers, Flat-Nosed Pliers

MATERIALS

7	assorted large crystal beads from 7mm to 10mm
270	smaller crystal beads from 3mm to 6mm
12	12" strands of size 13/0 gold-plated charlotte seed beads
100	2.5mm hollow gold-filled round beads
75	4mm vermeil daisy spacers
1	16mm vermeil ring of a toggle clasp (You do not need the toggle bar.)
1	12mm vermeil cones
20	gold-filled crimp beads
16'	of beading wire

NOTE
I have used two effective methods to fit all seven strands neatly into the cone. To make this work, you must attach the beading wire strands before adding the beads.

the hole of the large crystal bead and up through the crimp bead. Make sure all the beads fit snugly, close the crimp, and snip off the remaining tail of the wire.

4. Repeat this process for each of the other six strands. As you add beads to a strand, compare it with the ones you have already completed. Stagger the crystal beads so they create a pleasing effect. Make each of the strands a different length between approximately 22" and 24". To wear the necklace, simply put it around your neck and drop the ends of the strands through the toggle ring one at a time.

MULTI-STRAND CRYSTALS AND CHARLOTTES NECKLACE

CHARLOTTES ARE TINY SEED BEADS THAT HAVE A SINGLE FLAT FACET THAT IS CUT IN THE MANUFACTURING PROCESS AS THE LONG TUBE IS DRAWN OUT. THEY ARE SOMETIMES CALLED ONE-CUT SEED BEADS. BY COMBINING THESE BEADS WITH CRYSTALS IN MULTIPLE STRANDS, YOU CAN MAKE THE MOST OF THEIR FACETS. THE BEADS MAY BE TINY, BUT TOGETHER THEY CAN CREATE A LOT OF GLITTER AND SPARKLE.

TOOLS
Wire Cutters, Crimping Pliers, Flat-Nosed Pliers

MATERIALS

260	3mm Swarovski crystal bicones with AB coating
10	12" strands of size 13/0 gold plated charlottes (one-cut seed beads)
1	16mm vermeil toggle clasp
2	11mm vermeil cones
2	6mm gold-filled rings
2	4mm gold-filled jump rings
2"	of 20 gauge gold-filled wire
12'	of beading wire

1. To make one of the doubled strands, start with 36" of beading wire. Fold it in half. Pass the folded V-shaped end of the wire through a crimp, and attach it to one of the 6mm rings. Now, string on your crystals and charlottes. The pattern is quite random—use your own judgment of how to mix the beads or refer to the photograph for guidance. When you have a completed strand 16" long, put transparent tape around the end of the beading wire to keep the beads from falling off. Then, fill the other side of the doubled wire with crystals and charlottes. This time make the strand 16" long. Now, holding the two wire ends so that the beads can't fall off, remove the tape and insert

There are seven strands in all—five single and two double. Each end of the strand is attached to one of the six-millimeter rings. One pair of rings holds three single strands; the other pair holds the two doubled strands. The tops of the rings are squeezed into a pointed shape that fits snugly inside the cones. The wire is used to hold the pointed tops of the squeezed rings and is passed through the cones to secure everything to the clasp.

both ends into a crimp bead. Bring the wire through another 6mm ring and then back through the crimp. Before you squeeze the crimp shut, it is very important that you adjust the wires so the beads are all snug, with no gaps between them. Remember: The first wire is going to be a little shorter than the second, so tighten accordingly.

2.   For the first single strand, cut a 20" piece of beading wire. Attach one end to the same ring as that of the doubled strand, and fill it with crystals and charlottes to a length of 16$\frac{1}{2}$". Make sure all the beads are snug; attach the strand to the other 6mm ring (next to the doubled strand). Repeat this for the two remaining single strands.

3.   Stretch out the two multi-strands, making sure that the ends of the individual strands are all clustered together at the bottom of each ring. Use the flat-nosed pliers to gently squeeze the tops of the rings (that is, the parts of the rings furthest from the ends of the strands) until they are pointed enough to fit inside the cones.

4.   Cut the gold-filled wire in half. Pass the end of one piece through the pointed ends of two rings; secure them with a wire-wrapped loop. Now, add a cone to the wire so it sits down on the rings, covering the ends of every strand. Tug the end of the wire to make sure the fit is snug; make a wire-wrapped loop at the top of the cone. Use a 4mm jump ring to secure this loop to the clasp. Repeat this step to attach the other side of the necklace to the clasp.

BLOWN GLASS NECKLACE

THESE LOVELY BLOWN GLASS BEADS OFFER A CHALLENGE TO THE JEWELRY DESIGNER BECAUSE THE STRINGING MATERIAL IS VERY VISIBLE INSIDE THE BEAD. FORTUNATELY, ANOTHER ASPECT OF THE BEADS HELPS SOLVE THIS PROBLEM: SINCE THEY ARE BLOWN FROM TUBES OF GLASS, THESE BEADS TEND TO HAVE HOLES LARGE ENOUGH TO FIT A 2MM SILVER BEAD. BY COVERING THE BEADING WIRE WITH SMALL SILVER BEADS, THE HOLLOW GLASS IS FILLED WITH THE ATTRACTIVE SPARKLE OF SILVER, TURNING THE PROBLEM OF VISIBLE WIRE INTO AN OPPORTUNITY FOR INTERESTING DESIGN.

1. Start the necklace by threading on a crimp. Pass the beading wire through the ring of one half of the clasp and then back through the crimp. Make sure the beading wire is tight around the ring. Squeeze the crimp shut.

2. Thread on one 3mm bead and three 2mm silver beads.

3. Add a 3mm bead, an 8mm rondel, a 3mm bead, and six 2mm beads. Add a blown glass bead so that it fits over all the 2mm beads. Repeat this pattern eighteen times.

4. Check the necklace around your neck to make sure that its length is right. Add a 3mm bead, a glass rondel, a 3mm bead, three 2mm beads, a 3mm bead, and a crimp. Pass the beading wire through the ring of the other half of the toggle clasp and then back through the crimp. Tighten the necklace so there are no spaces between the beads, close the crimp, and snip off any remaining beading wire. Add the crimp covers.

TOOLS
Wire Cutters, Crimping Pliers

MATERIALS

19	12mm blown glass beads
20	8mm rondel glass beads
42	3mm silver hollow seamless round beads
120	2mm silver hollow seamless round beads
1	14mm silver toggle clasp
2	silver crimp beads
2	silver crimp bead covers
20"	of beading wire

HINT:
The smaller silver beads must fit though the holes of the blown glass beads, while the larger ones must be too big to go through. If 2mm or 3mm silver beads do not work, adjust the sizes to fit the blown glass bead holes. If you want to give this necklace extra security, add four mini-crimps spaced out on the necklace, each between a large silver bead and a small one.

LAMPWORK AND PRESSED GLASS BRACELET

DISC-SHAPED BEADS ARE OFTEN IDEAL FOR BRACELETS. THEY CREATE A BROAD BAND OF COLOR AROUND THE WRIST AND LAY FLATTER AND MORE COMFORTABLY THAN A SIMILAR-SIZED ROUND BEAD. THESE LOVELY LAMPWORK BEADS HAVE A PORCELAIN-LIKE QUALITY AND DEMONSTRATE HOW OPAQUE GLASS CAN BE USED TO GREAT EFFECT.

1. First, make the little dangle that will hang beside the clasp. Add a 3mm silver bead, a 6mm glass bead, and another silver 3mm bead to the headpin. Use the round-nosed pliers to make a loop at the top of the headpin, but do not close it completely. Slip the loop over the ring of the circular part of the toggle clasp and close it by wire-wrapping.

2. Thread a crimp onto the beading wire. Pass the beading wire through the ring of the same half of the clasp and then back through the crimp. Make sure the beading wire is tight around the ring. Squeeze the crimp shut. Thread on a silver bead, a disc bead, another silver bead, and a round glass bead. Repeat this pattern six times.

3. Try the bracelet on for size. Add a crimp. Bring the beading wire through the ring of the other side of the clasp and back through the crimp and the round bead. Now tighten the bracelet so there are no spaces between the beads, close the crimp, and snip off any remaining beading wire. Add the crimp covers.

TOOLS

Wire Cutters, Crimping Pliers, Round-Nosed Pliers, Flat-Nosed Pliers

MATERIALS (FOR A 7" BRACELET)

  7   15mm disc lampwork glass beads.

 .8   6mm round lampwork glass beads

 17   3mm silver hollow seamless round beads

  1   16mm silver toggle clasp

  2   silver crimp beads

  2   silver crimp bead covers

  1   1" silver headpin with ball end

10"   of silver beading wire

VINTAGE GLASS WITH GARNETS NECKLACE

THE WORD *VINTAGE* IS A BROADLY APPLIED DESCRIPTION IN THE WORLD OF GLASS BEADS. IN GENERAL, IT REFERS TO BEADS THAT WERE MADE AT SOME POINT IN THE EARLIER PART OF THE TWENTIETH CENTURY AND ARE NO LONGER BEING PRODUCED. IN THE CASE OF THESE SEEMINGLY SIMPLE VINTAGE BEADS, IT IS THE COLORS OF THE GLASS AND THE TECHNIQUE OF MIXING THEM THAT CREATE A UNIQUE LOOK, WELL DESERVING OF BEING MATCHED WITH SILVER AND GEMSTONE BEADS. THIS STYLE OF NECKLACE CAN BE WORN WITH THE CLASP EITHER IN FRONT, SO THAT THE SHORT STRAND IS A PENDANT, OR AS A CHOKER, WITH THE CLASP AND PENDANT AT THE BACK OF THE NECK.

1. Begin the necklace by passing the longer thread through the eye of the twisted wire needle. Double it and tie a knot at the end.

2. Using the instructions on page 130, attach a bead tip to the end of the thread. Add a 3mm round silver bead and a silver torus bead. Then, add a glass bead, a torus bead, a garnet bead, and another torus bead. Repeat this pattern 30 times. Add the 9mm silver bead and a 3mm silver bead. Finish off the strand by adding a clamshell bead tip. Use one of the niobium jump rings to attach the strand to the other half of the clasp.

3. Now, use the shorter piece of silk thread in the same manner to make the pendant. After adding the bead tip, add a 3mm silver bead, a torus bead, a garnet bead, and a torus. Then, add a glass bead, a torus bead, a garnet bead, and a torus bead. Repeat this pattern twice, add two 3mm beads, and finish off with another clamshell bead tip. Use a niobium jump ring to attach the first part of the strand to the large ring of the clasp.

4. Make the dangles by adding a 3mm bead, a torus bead, a glass bead, a 3mm silver bead, and a torus bead to each headpin. Finish them with a simple loop. Use the last jump ring to attach the dangles to the bottom end of the short strand.

FOR PRESSED GLASS BEADS, IT MIGHT BE THAT THE SHAPE IS UNUSUAL OR THAT THE ORIGINAL METAL MOLDS HAVE BEEN LOST OR DESTROYED. IN THE CASE OF CRYSTAL BEADS, THE COLOR MIGHT HAVE BEEN DROPPED FROM PRODUCTION, RESULTING IN RARE VALUE. LAMPWORK BEADS CAN BECOME VINTAGE WHEN THE TECHNIQUE BY WHICH THEY ARE MADE IS LOST OR THE COLOR OF THE GLASS IS NO LONGER AVAILABLE.

VINTAGE CAN MEAN SOMETHING DIFFERENT DEPENDING ON WHAT TYPES OF GLASS BEADS ARE BEING DISCUSSED.

TOOLS
Awl, Flat-Nosed Pliers, Twisted Wire Needle, Hypo-Cement or Clear Nail Polish

MATERIALS
- 31   9mm vintage lampwork glass beads
- 29   3.5mm round garnet beads
- 65   3.5mm silver torus-shaped spacer beads
- 3   5mm niobium jump rings
- 11   3mm silver seamless hollow round beads
- 6   9mm silver seamless hollow round beads
- 3   1" silver headpins with ball tips
- 1   13mm silver toggle clasp
- 2   silver clamshell bead tips
- 48"   of red size F silk thread cut into 36" and 12" pieces

SWAROVSKI CRYSTAL LARIAT

SWAROVSKI HAS BEEN A DRIVING FORCE IN GLASS JEWELRY FOR MANY YEARS. WITH FINISHED JEWELRY AND COMPONENTS DIVISIONS, AS WELL AS RETAIL STORES, SWAROVSKI HAS A STRONG UNDERSTANDING OF FASHION AND GOES TO GREAT LENGTHS TO BOTH FOLLOW AND INFLUENCE IT.

1. Cut a 4" piece from the beading wire. Thread a crimp onto this piece and add thirteen round crystal beads. Pass the wire through a 14mm donut and then back through the crimp. Arrange the beads so they make a nice tight loop around the edge of the donut. Push enough beading wire through the crimp so you can add another thirteen round beads. Pass this part of the wire through another 14mm donut and then back through the crimp again. Arrange the beads so they make a nice tight loop around the edge of the donut. Make sure both loops are well shaped and the beads are snug. With the beginning of the wire just through the crimp, squeeze the crimp firmly shut. Cut away the balance of the wire.

2. Repeat this process to add another 14mm donut to the last one.

3. Thread a crimp onto the remaining beading wire. Add seventeen round crystal beads. Pass the wire through the 20mm donut and then back through the crimp. Arrange the beads so they make a nice tight loop around the edge of the donut. When you are sure that all the beads are fitting snugly together, place the tail of the wire just through the crimp and squeeze the crimp shut.

4. Add about 23" of round crystal beads—but make sure you have thirteen beads left for the final loop. When you are happy with the length, add a crimp and the thirteen round crystal beads. Pass the wire through the end donut of the 14mm donut group and then back through the crimp. Arrange the beads so they make a nice tight loop around the edge of the donut. When all the beads in the necklace are snug against one another, squeeze the crimp shut. Add the crimp covers. To wear this lariat, simply double the strand back through the large ring.

EVERY YEAR, SWAROVSKI PRODUCES NEW COMPONENT DESIGNS, ONE OF WHICH IS THE RECENTLY INTRODUCED CRYSTAL RING, OR DONUT SHAPE. WITH ALL THE OUTSIDE EDGES, THE DONUT PROVIDES A GLITTERING ACCOMPANIMENT TO OTHER CRYSTAL BEADS AND WORKS PARTICULARLY WELL AS THE LINKING COMPONENT OF A LARIAT NECKLACE. BOTH TYPES OF CRYSTAL ARE IN THE CRYSTAL COPPER COLOR, BUT A DOZEN OTHER COLORS COULD BE USED TO SIMILAR EFFECT.

TOOLS
Wire Cutters, Crimping Pliers

MATERIALS
1   20mm Swarovski donut
3   14mm Swarovski donuts
540   2mm round Swarovski crystal beads (style 5000)
4   gold-filled crimp beads
4   gold-filled bead covers
35"   of beading wire

TUTTI BUMPS AND DOTS BRACELET

ALTHOUGH NO ONE BEAD IN THIS BRACELET IS THE SAME COLOR AS ANOTHER, THE DESIGN IS NOT SIMPLY RANDOM. THE BEADS HAVE A COMMON PATTERN OF BUMPS OR DOTS. THE BUMPY BEADS ARE OPPOSITE ONE ANOTHER, AS ARE THE DOTTY BEADS. TO ADD EVEN MORE BALANCE, THE DISC-SHAPED CENTER BEAD IS MATCHED BY A SIMILARLY SIZED DISC-SHAPED TOGGLE CLASP ON THE OPPOSITE SIDE. SO EVEN THOUGH THE OVERALL EFFECT IS ONE OF PLAYFUL, RANDOM COLOR, THERE REMAINS AN UNDERLYING SYMMETRY.

1. Thread a crimp onto the beading wire. Pass the last ring of the same half of the clasp back through the crimp. Make sure that the beading wire is tight around the ring. Squeeze the crimp shut. Thread on a round silver bead, 3 seed beads , a daisy spacer bead, a round bumpy bead, a daisy bead, 3 seed beads, a daisy bead, a round dotty glass bead, a daisy bead, 3 seed beads, a daisy bead, a glass dichroic bead with a bumpy edge, a daisy bead, 3 seed beads, a daisy bead, a round dotty bead, a daisy bead, 3 seed beads, a daisy bead, a round silver bead, a daisy bead, and the large glass disc bead.

2. Starting at the daisy bead/round silver bead/daisy bead combination, reverse the pattern above to make the other side of the bracelet. As you go, periodically check to make sure each type of bead sits opposite the same type of bead on the other side of the bracelet.

3. Try the bracelet on for size. Add a crimp. Bring the beading wire through the ring of the other side of the clasp and then back through the crimp and round bead. Now, tighten the bracelet so there are no spaces between the beads, close the crimp, and snip off any remaining beading wire. Add the crimp covers.

TOOLS
Wire Cutters, Crimping Pliers

MATERIALS: (FOR A 7" BRACELET)

4	11mm round lampwork glass beads with dot pattern
2	12mm flat disc lampwork glass beads with bumpy edges
2	12mm round lampwork glass beads with bumps
1	15mm flat disc lampwork glass bead with dot pattern
30	size 8/0 black seed beads
18	4mm silver daisy spacer beads
4	3mm silver hollow seamless round beads
1	14mm silver toggle clasp with large decorated rim
2	silver crimp beads
2	silver crimp bead covers
10"	of beading wire

TRIANGLE LAMPWORK BEAD BRACELET

TRIANGULAR BEADS CAN BE USED VERY EFFECTIVELY IN BRACELETS. ONE OF THE FLAT SURFACES SITS VERY COMFORTABLY AGAINST THE WRIST, WHILE THE APEX OF THE TRIANGLE FORMS A PROMINENT PYRAMID. THE VIBRANT, CONTEMPORARY COLORS OF THESE BOHEMIAN LAMPWORK BEADS, DESIGNED BY ALENA CHLADKOVA, ATTRACT IMMEDIATE ATTENTION. THE NICELY COLORED RED PRESSED GLASS BEADS ARE CALLED DRUKS BY THE CZECHS, A WORD DESCRIBING ANY PLAIN-COLORED AND UNDECORATED ROUND PRESSED GLASS BEAD. DESPITE THEIR LUMPY SOUNDING NAME, DRUKS ARE BOTH IMMENSELY USEFUL AS SPACERS AND, IN THE RIGHT COLOR, ELEGANTLY SIMPLE.

1. Thread a crimp onto the beading wire. Pass the wire through the ring of the same half of the clasp and then back through the crimp. Make sure that the beading wire is tight around the ring. Squeeze the crimp shut. Thread on a silver daisy spacer bead, a 4mm round glass bead, another silver daisy, and an opaque triangle bead. Repeat this pattern 6 more times, but make the second, fourth, and sixth triangle beads transparent ones.

2. Try the bracelet around your wrist for size. Add a silver daisy, a round bead, another daisy, and a crimp. Bring the beading wire through the ring of the other side of the clasp and then back through the crimp and the round bead. Now, tighten the bracelet so there are no spaces between the beads, close the crimp, and snip off any remaining beading wire. Add the crimp covers.

TOOLS
Wire Cutters, Crimping Pliers

MATERIALS (FOR AN 8" BRACELET)

4	16mm x 14mm triangular lampwork glass beads in an opaque base color
3	16mm x 14mm triangular lampwork glass beads in a transparent base color
8	6mm round pressed glass beads
16	4mm silver daisy spacer beads
1	16mm silver toggle clasp
2	silver crimp beads
2	silver crimp bead covers
10"	of beading wire

CRYSTAL AND SILVER CHAIN NECKLACE

BLUES AND GREENS TEND TO GO WELL WITH SILVER: THESE ARE THE PREDOMINANT COLORS IN THIS NECKLACE. I HAVE USED A SMALLER NUMBER OF AMBER TONES TO ADD A LITTLE WARMTH TO THE DESIGN. EACH ONE OF THE OCTAGONAL CRYSTAL BEADS IS LARGE AND IMPRESSIVE AND BALANCES WELL AGAINST THE LARGE LINKS OF THE HEAVY SILVER CHAIN. THE SHAPE OF THE LINKS IS SIMILAR TO THAT OF THE BEADS AND CREATES A HARMONIOUS APPEARANCE—A SIMPLE DESIGN TO BE SURE, BUT ONE THAT IS ELEGANT AND DISTINGUISHED.

1. Start by attaching each of the crystal beads to a piece of looped wire in the following way: Use your round-nosed pliers to make a simple loop at one end of the silver wire. Thread a silver torus bead onto the wire and then add a crystal bead and another silver bead. Make sure the beads are snug against one another and against the loop; then, cut the wire about ¼" above the last bead. Make a simple loop, ensuring that the bottom of the loop fits tightly against the round bead. Repeat this process for the rest of the silver and crystal beads.

2. Cut the chain into thirteen pieces; each piece should be three links long.

3. Attach a crystal bead to the end of a piece of chain by opening the loop, slipping it on the end link of the piece of chain, and then closing it. Attach the next crystal bead to the other end of the chain. Continue adding beads and chain until you have used them all.

4. Add the last piece of chain to the end crystal bead. Use the jump rings to attach half of the clasp to each end of the necklace.

TOOLS
Wire Cutters, Round-Nosed, and Flat-Nosed Pliers

MATERIALS
- 12   18mm x 10mm Swarovski crystal beads
- 24   4mm silver torus spacer beads
- 28"   of silver chain with heavy 11mm x 7mm links (or enough for 13 sections of 3 links each when cut)
- 15"   20 gauge silver wire
- 1   22mm x 13mm oval toggle clasp

SILVER AND CRYSTAL HOOP EARRINGS

USING HOOP EARWIRES IS ONE OF THE SIMPLEST WAYS TO MAKE EARRINGS—JUST ADD A FEW CRYSTALS, AND THEY ARE GOOD TO GO. THESE CRYSTAL DROPS ARE JUST AS EASY TO USE AS ROUNDS BUT GIVE A LITTLE EXTRA DIMENSION TO THE DESIGN.

1. Add a round silver bead and then a crystal drop to the hoop. Repeat twelve times and add a final silver bead.

2. Use the flat-nosed piers to bend ¼" of the straight end of the hoop wire into a right angle so it will catch in the looped end to close the earring.

TOOLS
Flat-Nosed Pliers

MATERIALS
- 26 6mm x 4mm Swarovski crystal top-drilled drops
- 28 2mm hollow silver round beads
- 2 1" silver hoop earwires

CRYSTAL AND VERMEIL EARRINGS

VERMEIL IS A WONDERFUL MATERIAL, MUCH LESS EXPENSIVE THAN GOLD BUT AS VALUABLE AND DURABLE AS PRECIOUS METAL. FOR THESE EARRINGS, THE EARWIRE, OR STUD, IS AS MUCH A PART OF THE DESIGN AS THE CRYSTAL. THE LARGE ROUND GOLDEN SHAPE COUNTERBALANCES THE LARGER OF THE CRYSTAL BEADS.

1. Add an 8mm crystal bead, a bead cap with its convex side facing the bead, a 4mm crystal, and a 2mm gold bead to a headpin.

2. Make a simple loop above the last bead. Open the loop, attach it to the ring of the ear stud, and then close.

TOOLS
Round-Nosed Pliers, Flat-Nosed Pliers

MATERIALS
- 2 8mm round Swarovski crystal beads
- 2 4mm bicone Swarovski crystal beads
- 2 5mm Bali-style vermeil bead caps
- 2 2mm hollow gold-filled round beads
- 2 1" gold-filled headpins
- 2 vermeil ear studs with 8mm diameter faces

GOLD AND CRYSTAL HOLIDAY SPARKLE EARRINGS

SPACER BARS, WHEN THEY ARE LINKED TOGETHER WITH JUMP RINGS, CAN CREATE A CHAIN-LIKE EFFECT.

1. Start the earring by making all the little crystal dangles. Add a 1.5mm gold charlotte bead, a crystal, and another 1.5mm gold bead to each $1/2$" headpin; make a simple loop.

2. Open the jump rings. Add three dangles to a jump ring and then hook it to one ring of the chain. Close the jump ring. Repeat this to add three dangles to each of the other rings.

3. Open the loop of the earwire and add the end of the chain. Add three dangles to a jump ring and close. Add that jump ring to the open earwire loop and then close.

TOOLS
Round-Nose Pliers, Flat-Nose Pliers

MATERIALS

24 3mm bicone Swarovski crystal beads with 2xAB coating

48 size 11/0 gold-plated charlotte seed beads

2 $1^1/_8$" pieces of gold-filled "long and short" chain, each with 3 long bars and 3 rings

8 3mm gold-filled jump rings

24 $1/2$" gold-filled headpins with ball tip

1 pair gold-filled earwires

CRYSTAL AND GOLD CHAIN EARRINGS

DECORATING CHAIN LINKS WITH BEADS IS AN ATTRACTIVE WAY
TO CREATE LONG EARRINGS. HERE, THE CHAIN LINKS ARE LARGE
CIRCLES THAT PROVIDE INTERESTING FRAMES FOR THE LITTLE
CRYSTAL DANGLES.

1. Start the earring by making the 30 little crystal dangles. Add a crystal bead to each $\frac{1}{2}$" headpin. Make a simple loop.

2. Open a jump ring and add three of the dangles and close. Open the loop of the earwire and attach the jump ring with the three dangles and the end link of a piece of the chain. Close the loop.

3. Add three dangles to the second link of the chain by opening and closing the loops of the dangles. Add another three dangles to the fourth, the sixth, and the last links of the chain.

TOOLS
Round-Nosed Pliers, Flat-Nosed Pliers,
Wire Cutters

MATERIALS

30	4mm Swarovski crystal bicone beads (Style 5301)
30	$\frac{1}{2}$" gold-filled headpins with ball tips
2	4mm gold-filled jump rings
30	2mm hollow gold-filled round beads
2	8-link sections of gold-filled circle chain with 10mm links (about 3" each)
2	gold-filled earwires

GLASS AS GOOD AS GOLD EARRINGS

THE PRECISE CUTS AND HIGHLY POLISHED SURFACES OF CRYSTAL GLASS CAN BE SPECTACULAR WHEN THEY ARE COATED. IN THESE EARRINGS, THE SWAROVSKI CRYSTAL BICONES ARE DOUBLE-PLATED WITH REAL GOLD, CREATING WONDERFULLY REFLECTIVE FACETS. THE BEADS WILL THUS APPEAR THE SAME AS, BUT WEIGH LESS THAN, REAL GOLD. AND WHO COULD TELL THE DIFFERENCE BETWEEN THESE LITTLE GLASS JEWELS AND THE REAL THING?

1. Start the earrings by making the sixteen dangles. Add a crystal bead and a round bead to a headpin; then, make a simple loop. Repeat until you have made all sixteen dangles.

2. Cut the chain so you have two equal pieces, each with seven links. Attach the end link of the chain to the loop of an earwire. Open the loops of the dangles slightly by bending the wire sideways at the joint. Add one dangle to the loop of the earwire. Add one dangle to the bottom of each link of the chain.

TOOLS
Wire Cutters, Round-Nosed Pliers

MATERIALS
- 16   4mm Swarovski crystal Aurum bicone beads (5301)
- 16   2mm gold-filled hollow seamless round beads
- 16 $1/2$" vermeil headpins
- 2   vermeil earwires
- 5"   of gold-filled chain with 10mm circular links (or enough for 14 links)

VENETIAN GLASS NECKLACE

VENICE IS THE GREAT HISTORICAL CENTER OF GLASS BEAD-MAKING. ALTHOUGH THE AMOUNT OF GLASS PRODUCED THERE IS NOW RELATIVELY SMALL, VENICE'S PRODUCTS AND DESIGN INNOVATIONS ARE AS GREAT AS EVER, CONSEQUENTLY DRIVING UP THE PRICE OF GENUINE VENETIAN GLASS. SADLY, FEW VISITORS TO VENICE EVER SEE REAL VENETIAN GLASS BEADS, AS TOURIST SHOPS AND EVEN SPECIALTY BEAD STORES HAVE TAKEN TO SELLING FAR CHEAPER COPIES FROM THE CZECH REPUBLIC, CHINA, AND INDIA. WHILE THE FOREIGN COPIES ARE SOMETIMES VERY, VERY GOOD, NOTHING COMPARES TO THAT INEFFABLE QUALITY THAT SEEMS TO BE THE VERY HEART OF THE VENETIAN STYLE.

THE BEADS IN THIS NECKLACE SEEM SO SIMPLE—GOLD FOIL WRAPPED IN FROSTED, TRANSLUCENT ITALIAN GLASS. YET BOTH THEIR TEXTURE AND THEIR COLOR ARE PERFECTLY DELIGHTFUL, AND NO ONE WILL EVER MISTAKE THEM FOR ANYTHING LESS THAN THE VALUABLE VENETIAN GLASS BEADS THEY ARE. IT IS SAID THAT TRULY AUTHENTIC ITALIAN CUISINE DOES NOT TRAVEL ONE METER OUTSIDE THE BORDER OF ITALY; VENICE'S TALENT FOR PRODUCING UNIQUELY DELICIOUS BEADS LIKEWISE REMAINS REMOTE.

1. Make a simple loop at one end of the gold-filled wire. Add a bead cap (convex side facing the loop); then, add a glass bead and another bead cap (concave side facing the bead). Cut the wire about $1/4$" above the bead cap, and make a simple loop. Repeat this procedure with the rest of the glass beads and bead caps.

2. Use the 5mm split rings to join all of the wired glass beads together in a chain; then, add a 7mm split ring to each end. Attach the hook clasp to one of the 7mm split rings.

TOOLS

Wire Cutters, Crimping Pliers, Round-Nosed Pliers, Flat-Nosed Pliers

MATERIALS:

24	12mm round Venetian lampwork glass beads with interior gold foil
48	4mm gold-filled beads caps
24	5mm gold-filled split rings
2	7mm gold-filled split rings
1	16mm vermeil hook clasp
24"	of 20 gauge gold-filled wire

VENETIAN GLASS EARRINGS

THESE GLASS BEADS, LIKE THE BEADS USED IN THE VENETIAN GLASS NECKLACE, ENCASE REAL GOLD FOIL. THE LITTLE BEAD CAPS AND FINDINGS ARE GOLD-FILLED, LEADING ONE TO BELIEVE THAT THE ELEGANT EARWIRE IS GOLD TOO. HOWEVER, THIS UNIQUE SHAPE WOULD BE HEAVY AND EXPENSIVE IF IT WERE MADE OF SOLID GOLD; RATHER, IT IS MADE OF BEAUTIFULLY PLATED PEWTER EARWIRE FROM TIERRACAST.

1. To a headpin, add a bead cap with the convex side facing the head of the headpin, an 8mm glass bead, and a 3mm gold bead. Cut the headpin to leave about $1/4$" above the last bead and make a simple loop.

2. Make a loop at the end of the wire and add a bead cap (convex side facing the loop), a 10mm glass bead, and another bead cap (concave side facing the bead). Cut the wire $1/4$" above the bead cap and make a simple loop. Repeat this with a 12mm glass bead.

3. Open a loop and attach the 8mm bead section to the 10mm bead section; then, attach the 10mm bead section to the 12mm bead section. Finally open the jump ring and use it to attach the 12mm bead section to the earwire. Make sure you close all the loops.

TOOLS
Round-Nosed Pliers, Flat-Nosed Pliers, Wire Cutters

MATERIALS:
- 2 12mm frosted round Venetian beads with interior gold foil
- 2 10mm frosted round Venetian beads with interior gold foil
- 2 8mm frosted round Venetian beads with interior gold foil
- 10 4.5mm gold-filled bead caps
- 2 3mm hollow gold-filled round beads
- 5" of 20 gauge gold-filled wire
- 2 1" gold-filled headpins
- 2 5mm oval gold-filled jump rings
- 2 gold-plated pewter earwires

TOUCHES OF GLASS

DESIGNING WITH OTHER BEADS

Glass beads are used across the entire range of jewelry, from the simple and inexpensive to the complex and costly. Not only do glass beads come in endless varieties, but their quality and value are defined by artistic merit rather than by base material; thus, it is impossible to form sweeping generalizations about which types of beads go well with which kinds of glass. The truth is that you can find a glass bead to match pretty much any jewelry component.

In this book, it is the glass beads that have dictated the choice of companion materials, a decision that was made by considering not only the color, pattern, and size of the beads but also the quality of both their design and their craftsmanship. In general, the better the bead, the finer the supporting components should be. When choosing findings and spacer beads, use the following guide.

COMBINE WITH GOLD:

The finest, most expensive lampwork glass beads
Antique glass beads
Glass beads of great artistic merit

COMBINE WITH GOLD-FILLED, VERMEIL, AND SILVER:

Fine-quality lampwork glass beads
Crystal beads
Dichroic glass beads
Very good quality and unusual pressed glass beads

COMBINE WITH PLATED BASE METAL AND PLATED PLASTIC:

Ordinary pressed-glass beads
Inexpensive and lesser-quality lampwork glass beads

Do not hesitate to combine gemstones and glass. Many glass beads are considerably more expensive and much more beautiful than many gemstone beads. Glass beads can also support, or be supported by, all of the organics, such as wood, bone, and resin.

Whatever companion materials you use, it is essential to create a sense of harmony among the individual components. For a jewelry designer, this means trying to balance size, color, shape, and texture.

Size is a primary consideration: Do you want one component to simply show off the other, or do you want all of the beads to command equal attention? Even when the beads are all of equal importance to the jewelry, you can easily achieve a sense of proportion by making all the beads a similar size; it is equally effective, however (and often more interesting), to use several smaller beads to counterbalance each large bead.

Shape, texture, and reflection are also important. A complex shape or pattern is bound to win more attention than a plain round bead. Texture usually wins out when set alongside a smoother surface. Yet even a plain, smooth surface can sometimes trump pattern and texture—if it is highly reflective. In jewelry, it is often sparkle that takes first prize.

Color plays a large part in the equation. Bright, vivid colors simply attract the eye more than those that are paler and more subdued. Because glass beads offer a limitless range of color combinations, they can always be made to play either the leading or the supporting role with other materials.

Here are some very general suggestions for combining colors, although changing fashion and individual taste create numerous exceptions.

SOME PLEASANT COLOR COMBINATIONS:
Blue and green
Red and brown
Red and yellow
Blue and gray
Yellow and green
Pink and purple
Green and pink
Red and blue
Brown and yellow

COLORS THAT GO PARTICULARLY WELL WITH GOLD:
Red
Pink
Purple
Green
Amber

COLORS THAT GO PARTICULARLY WELL WITH SILVER:
Blue
Black
Gray
Amethyst
Violet
Green

GLASS AND SILVER EYEGLASS LEASH

THIS STYLE OF EYEGLASS LEASH USES A SPECIAL FINDING IN THE SHAPE OF A LARGE SILVER RING INTO WHICH ONE ARM OF THE EYEGLASSES WILL SLIP. BECAUSE IT ALLOWS THE LEASH TO DOUBLE AS A NECKLACE, IT IS AN INTERESTING ALTERNATIVE TO THE STYLE IN WHICH THE LEASH IS ATTACHED TO EACH END OF THE GLASSES. THE LOVELY SHAPE OF THIS EYEGLASS HOLDER AND THE LITTLE DANGLE ON THE CLASP, MAKES THIS AN INTERESTING PIECE OF JEWELRY, EVEN WITHOUT THE EYEGLASSES.

THE LARGE GLASS BEADS IN THIS DESIGN ARE PRESSED GLASS MADE FROM A ROD OF MIXED COLOR, GIVING THEM A VERY NATURAL LOOK. THE RATHER IRREGULAR SEED BEADS ARE ALSO DRAWN FROM A MIXED BATCH OF GLASS. BOTH COULD EASILY BE MISTAKEN FOR TURQUOISE AND EXHIBIT A GEMLIKE QUALITY THAT MATCHES PERFECTLY WITH THE TINY SOLID SILVER "CHIPS." SOMETIMES GLASS MIMICS GEMSTONE SO WELL THAT IT LOOKS BETTER THAN THE STONE ITSELF!

1. First, make the little dangle that will hang beside the clasp. Add two silver chips, an 8mm glass bead, another silver chip, a seed bead, and one more silver chip to a headpin. Finish it off with a small loop.

2. Using a crimp bead, attach the beading wire to one of the loops of the eyeglass holder. The pattern of the beads is random, so you should feel free to vary it. To copy my pattern exactly, add 3S, 3SC, 1S, 4SC, one 8mm bead, 1SC, 3S, 1SC, 1S, 1SC, 3S, 3SC, 1S, 1SC,1S,1SC, 1S, 4SC, 1S, 1SC, one 8mm bead, 3SC, 1S, 2SC, one 8mm bead, 5SC, one 8mm bead, 1SC, 9S, 1SC, 1S, 1SC, 1S, 4SC, 1S, 1SC, one 8mm bead, 3S, 2SC, 1S, 7SC, 2S, 1SC, 3S, 6SC, 5S, 2SC, 1S, 1SC, one 8mm bead, 1SC, 3S, 1SC, 1S, 3SC, 1S, 1SC, 1S, 1SC, one 8mm bead,1SC, 2S, one 5mm bead, 3SC, 1S, 1SC, 7S, 7SC, 1S, 3SC, 3S, 3SC, 1S, 3SC, 6S, 3SC, 1S, 1SC, 1S, 3SC, one 8mm bead, 1SC, 2S, 3SC, one 8mm bead, 1SC, one 8mm bead, 5, S, 3SC, 1S, 3SC, 3S, one 5mm bead, 1S, 4SC, 1S, one 8mm bead, 1SC, 1S, 3SC, 1S, 4SC, 4S, 1SC, one 8mm bead, 1SC, 1S, 7SC, 3S, and 4SC. Add a crimp. Thread the wire through the loop of the spring clasp and then back through the crimp. Make sure all the beads are snug on the wire. Close the crimp. Trim the end of the wire.

3. Open a jump ring and slip on the dangle. Close the jump ring and slip it onto the open spring ring clasp.

TOOLS
Wire Cutters, Crimping Pliers, Flat-Nosed Pliers, Round-Nosed Pliers

MATERIALS (FOR A 20" LEASH)
- 13 8mm glass beads
- 96 size 6/0 seed beads (S)
- 137 (approximately) 3mm–7mm Thai silver "chips" (SC)
- 1 20mm silver eyeglass holder
- 2 5mm silver beads
- 1 6mm silver jump ring
- 1 5mm silver spring ring clasp
- 1 1" silver headpin with ball end
- 2 silver crimp beads
- 2 silver crimp bead covers
- 24" of beading wire

CAPPED LAMPWORK GLASS WITH SEED BEADS NECKLACE

GLASS BEADS CAN BE PLATED WITH SILVER, GOLD, AND OTHER METALS THROUGH CHEMICAL AND ELECTROLYTIC METHODS. SINCE THE PLATING IS REAL SILVER, THESE CYLINDER BEADS FORM A CHAIN OF ALMOST SOLID SILVER BROKEN ONLY BY THE GLASS BEADS. THE LARGE SILVER CAPS ADD TO THE OVERALL LOOK OF PRECIOUS METAL EVEN THOUGH THE NECKLACE IS MOSTLY GLASS. THE LAMPWORK BEADS ARE A SUBTLE COMBINATION OF AN AMETHYST CORE AND SURROUNDING LIGHT BLUE; MANY OTHER COLORS, HOWEVER, WOULD ALSO WORK WELL WITH THIS DESIGN.

1. Thread a crimp onto the beading wire. Pass the beading wire through the ring of one half of the clasp and then back through the crimp. Make sure that the beading wire is tight around the ring. Squeeze the crimp shut. Thread on a round silver bead, nine seed beads, another round silver bead, a bead cap (convex side facing the seed beads), and a lampwork glass bead. Repeat this pattern seven times.

2. Add a bead cap (concave side facing the last bead); then, add a round silver bead, nine seed beads, a round silver bead, and a lampwork glass bead. Repeat this pattern six times. Try the necklace on to check the length; then, finish off with a round silver bead, nine seed beads, and another round silver bead. Add a crimp and bring the beading wire through the ring of the other side of the clasp and then back through the crimp and the round silver bead. Now, tighten the necklace so there are no spaces between the beads, close the crimp, and snip off any remaining beading wire. Add the crimp covers.

TOOLS
Wire Cutters, Crimping Pliers

MATERIALS (FOR AN 18" NECKLACE)

15	10mm two-toned lampwork glass beads
16	10mm silver-plated Tierracast bead caps
144	2mm silver-plated cylinder beads (these are Delicas)
32	2.5mm silver hollow seamless round beads
1	12mm silver toggle clasp
2	silver crimp beads
2	silver crimp bead covers
20"	of silver beading wire

LAMPWORK GLASS WITH PEWTER NECKLACE

BECAUSE THESE LOVELY LAMPWORK GLASS BEADS BY NANCY PILGRIM ARE "FUMED," OR SMOKED WITH MICROSCOPIC GOLD FILM, THEY CALL FOR A GOLD ACCOMPANIMENT. BUT WHAT DO YOU DO IF YOUR BUDGET DOES NOT ALLOW FOR GOLD-FILLED OR VERMEIL BEADS? THE ANSWER IS GOLD-PLATED PEWTER, AN ALLOY COMPOSED MAINLY OF TIN. THE INTERESTING SHAPE OF THE LITTLE PEWTER CHARMS DRAMATICALLY CHANGES THE LOOK OF THE NECKLACE AND ENHANCES THE APPEARANCE OF THE GLASS RONDELS.

1. Thread a crimp onto the beading wire. Pass the beading wire through the ring of one half of the clasp and then back through the crimp. Make sure that the beading wire is tight around the ring. Squeeze the crimp shut. Thread on a 2.5mm bead, a 3mm bead, a 6mm glass bead, a 3mm bead, a 2.5mm bead, and another 3mm bead.

2. Add a 12mm rondel, a 3mm bead, a 2.5mm bead, a pewter charm, a 2.5mm, and a 3mm bead. Repeat the pattern twenty-four times.

3. Try the necklace on for size. Add a 3mm bead, a 2.5mm bead, a 3mm bead, a 6mm glass bead, a 3mm bead, a 2.5mm bead, and a crimp. Bring the beading wire through the ring of the other side of the clasp and then back through the crimp and the round bead. Now, tighten the necklace so there are no spaces between the beads, close the crimp, and snip off any remaining beading wire. Add the crimp covers.

TOOLS
Wire Cutters, Crimping Pliers

MATERIALS
25	12mm rondel "fumed" lampwork glass beads
2	6mm lampwork glass beads
24	6mm x 10mm gold-plated pewter charms.
54	3mm gold-filled hollow seamless round beads
52	2.5mm gold-filled hollow seamless round beads
1	14mm gold-plated toggle clasp
2	gold-filled crimp beads
2	gold-filled bead covers
20"	of gold colored beading wire

ANTIQUE GLASS AND SILVER NECKLACE

BEADS ARE AMONG THE OLDEST DECORATIVE CREATIONS, AND GLASS BEADS ARE THE MOST VARIED AND INTERESTING. LIKE A CHARM BRACELET, ANTIQUE BEAD JEWELRY SHOULD BE MADE WITH PIECES YOU HAVE COLLECTED OVER THE YEARS. YOU CAN START WITH A BRACELET AND REMAKE IT INTO A NECKLACE AS YOUR COLLECTION INCREASES. HOW CAN YOU TELL IF A BEAD IS ANTIQUE? WELL, THE STYLE, COLOR, AND PATINA WILL GIVE YOU SOME CLUES, AS WILL THE REPUTATION OF THE SELLER. FORTUNATELY, MOST ANTIQUE BEAD PRICES HAVE NOT YET REACHED SOARING HEIGHTS (THUS MAKING THE PRODUCTION OF FAKES PROFITABLE), AND IT IS STILL POSSIBLE TO ACQUIRE AN INTERESTING COLLECTION AT A REASONABLE COST.

IN THIS NECKLACE, THERE ARE MOSTLY VENETIAN BEADS THAT WERE USED TO BARTER FROM THE SEVENTEENTH TO THE NINETEENTH CENTURIES—THE SO-CALLED AFRICAN TRADING BEADS. BUT THERE ARE ALSO OLD CHINESE GLASS BEADS, AS WELL AS A LARGE ANTIQUE SILVER BEAD. THE SILVER SPACER BEADS ARE MOSTLY GRANULATED OR DECORATED DESIGNS; THE TARNISHING OF THE SILVER GIVES AN ANTIQUE LOOK. THAI SILVER BEADS WOULD ALSO BE A GOOD CHOICE, AS THEY OFTEN HAVE A DULLER SURFACE, THAT MATCHES BETTER WITH THE AGED APPEARANCE OF THE MAIN BEADS.

1. First, arrange your beads on a bead board or soft fabric surface. For a graduated design like the one I have used here, select one large bead to be the central element; then, arrange the other main beads (not the spacers) in a declining order of size.

2. When you are happy with the arrangement, use a crimp to attach the clasp to the end of the wire and begin adding your beads. Since many antique beads have large holes, use the 3mm and 4mm beads to fit at the end of the hole. Seat the bead firmly on the wire. Add the spacer beads as you see fit.

3. Hold up the necklace to make sure the central bead is in the center and the length is what you want. Tighten the necklace so there are no spaces between the beads, close the crimp, and snip off any remaining beading wire. If you have a dangling silver bead, as I have here, you can use the jump ring to attach it to the wire next to the clasp.

TOOLS
Wire Cutters, Crimping Pliers

MATERIALS

31	assorted antique glass beads from 5mm to 22mm in size
10	assorted old silver beads from 6mm to 23mm in size
24	assorted silver spacer beads
16	4mm round frosted black glass beads
1	6mm silver jump rings
20	3mm silver hollow seamless round beads
1	14mm silver toggle clasp
2	silver crimp beads
2	silver bead covers
28"	of beading wire

ENAMEL CENTERPIECE NECKLACE

ENAMEL IS A GLASS-LIKE FILM FUSED TO A METAL, CERAMIC, OR GLASS BASE. TRADITIONAL, OR VITREOUS, ENAMEL IS PRODUCED WHEN POWDERED GLASS, OFTEN IN THE FORM OF A PASTE, IS HEATED TO A HIGH TEMPERATURE ON THE BASE MATERIAL TO PRODUCE A THIN LAYER OF SOLID GLASS. THIS TRADITIONAL ENAMEL CENTERPIECE IS BY SUSAN KNOPP.

1. Thread on a crimp. Pass the beading wire through the ring of one half of the clasp and back through the crimp. Make sure that the beading wire is tight around the ring. Squeeze the crimp shut.

2. Thread two 2.5mm beads, a 5mm Thai silver bead, and a dichroic bead. Now add a 2.5mm bead, a 5mm bead, a 2.5mm bead, a 10mm rondel, a 2.5mm bead, a 5mm bead, a 2.5mm bead, and a 12mm glass bead. Repeat this pattern (A) once more; then, add a 2.5mm bead, a 5mm bead, a 2.5mm bead, and a 12mm glass bead. Repeat this pattern (B) once more; then, add a 2.5mm bead, a 5mm bead, a 2.5mm bead, a dichroic bead, a 2.5mm bead, a 5mm bead, a 2.5mm bead, a 10mm rondel, a 2.5mm bead, a 5mm bead, a 2.5mm bead, and a dichroic bead. Repeat pattern B. Then, repeat pattern A twice. Add a 2.5mm bead, a 5mm bead, a 2.5mm bead, a dichroic bead, a 2.5mm bead, and a 5mm bead to complete the first side of the necklace.

3. Add the ten Thai silver chips and pass the wire through the top of the centerpiece. Complete the other side of the necklace as a mirror image of the first. Pass the beading wire through the ring of the other half of the toggle clasp and then back through the crimp. Now, tighten the necklace so there are no spaces between the beads, close the crimp, and snip off any remaining beading wire. Add the crimp covers.

4. To make the little dangle, add a dichroic bead, a 2.5mm bead, and a crystal bead to the 1" headpin. Make a wire-wrapped loop to attach to the bottom of the centerpiece. Add a crystal to each of the two $\frac{1}{2}$" headpins and make simple loops to attach them to the loop of the larger dangle.

TOOLS
Wire cutters, Crimping Pliers

MATERIALS

1	46mm enamel on silver centerpiece
14	12mm round lampwork with inside silver foil beads
10	10mm rondel lampwork with inside silver foil beads
9	8mm round dichroic beads
34	5mm Thai silver beads
10	3 to 4mm Thai silver chips
70	2.5mm silver hollow seamless round beads
3	2mm round crystal beads
2	$\frac{1}{2}$" silver headpins with ball tip
2	1" silver headpin with ball tip
1	24mm hook and eye clasp
1	silver crimp bead
1	silver crimp bead cover
22"	of beading wire

ITSY-BITSY BEADS AND VERMEIL NECKLACE

WORKING WITH THE TINIEST GLASS BEADS IS TIME CONSUMING AND EYE CHALLENGING. THE REWARD IS THAT YOU CAN PRODUCE FEATHER-LIGHT STRANDS OF EXTREME DELICACY. THIS NECKLACE USES THE SMALLEST OF SEED BEADS, SIZE 15/0 CHARLOTTES, AND AMAZING MINIATURE FACETED CRYSTALS ONLY TWO MILLIMETERS IN DIAMETER. AS SUBTLE AND AS LOVELY AS A VERY THIN STRAND CAN BE AROUND THE NECK, YOU CERTAINLY DON'T WANT IT TO GO UNNOTICED. HERE I HAVE USED SEVERAL METHODS TO INCREASE THE EFFECT OF THE VERY SMALL BEADS. THE STRAND IS COMPRISED OF FACETED GOLD-PLATED SEED BEADS AND FACETED CRYSTALS, GIVING IT LOTS OF SPARKLE. THE EXTREME LENGTH ALLOWS IT TO BE WRAPPED AROUND THE NECK TWO, THREE, OR EVEN FOUR TIMES, AND THE LEAFLIKE VERMEIL TRIANGLE CHARMS HAVE A BROAD REFLECTIVE SURFACE TO CATCH THE EYE.

1. Thread a crimp onto the beading wire; pass the wire through a jump ring and back through the crimp. Squeeze the crimp shut. Cut away any exposed tail from the wire. Start adding a mixture of charlottes and crystals to the wire. The pattern will be random, but the overall ratio should be about 3–4 charlottes to 1 crystal. Refer to the photograph for guidance.

2. After 5" or 6", add a pair of 2.5mm round gold beads. These will be the anchors for the vermeil triangles. Continue the charlotte/crystal combination for another 4"; then, add two more round gold beads. Continue in this way, adding a pair of round gold beads at intervals between 4" and 9". For rough guidance, the intervals I have used are 5", 4", 5", 6", 5", 4", 8", 4", 5½", 3", 5½", 6", 9", and 4".

3. When you have used all of your seed beads and crystals, add a crimp, pass the wire through the loop of the other side of the clasp and then back through the crimp, and squeeze shut. Snip off any excess wire and add the crimp covers.

4. Open a jump ring and hook on a vermeil triangle charm. Hook the jump ring over the beaded strand in between one of the pairs of gold 2.5mm beads and then close it shut. Repeat this with the rest of the jump rings and triangles, adding one to each of the 2.5mm gold bead pairs.

TOOLS
Wire Cutters, Crimping Pliers, Flat-Nosed Pliers

MATERIALS (FOR AN 86" ROPE)

455	2mm Swarovski crystal round beads in 3 assorted colors
5	12" strands of size 15/0 gold-plated charlottes (one-cut seed beads)
14	10mm vermeil flat triangle charms
28	2.5mm gold-filled hollow seamless round beads
14	5mm gold-filled jump rings
1	9mm vermeil toggle clasp
2	gold-filled crimp beads
2	gold-filled bead covers
7½'	of beading wire

PRESSED GLASS WITH SILVER TWO-STRAND NECKLACE

MODERN MACHINERY CAN HELP KEEP THE COST OF PRODUCING PRESSED GLASS BEADS RELATIVELY LOW, BUT THAT DOES NOT NECESSARILY MEAN THAT THESE "MACHINE-MADE" BEADS ALWAYS LOOK INEXPENSIVE. THE UNUSUAL SPIRAL BEAD SHAPE ADDS INTEREST TO THIS NECKLACE, WHILE THE SMALL THAI SILVER BEADS ADD A CERTAIN ELEGANCE THAT MAKES THE NECKLACE SOMETHING MUCH MORE THAN JUST "PRESSED GLASS."

1. Thread a crimp onto the beading wire. Pass the beading wire through the top rings of the clasp and then back through the crimp. Make sure that the beading wire is tight around the ring. Squeeze the crimp shut. Use the short strand pattern to thread on the beads. Attach the other end of the strand to the top ring of the other side of the clasp, cutting off the extra wire for the second strand.

2. Make the second strand in the same manner by attaching it to the lower rings of the clasp. Pause at the silver disc bead and hold the necklace to your neck to make sure the that the silver disc will fall in the center and that the second strand will hang below the first. Add or subtract beads if you need to adjust the proportion.

3. If you want to try to follow my design exactly, use the following patterns, which are based on the codes in the ingredients list:
    Short strand pattern—crimp, 2xe,j, c, i, d, e, d, e, a, j, b, j, b, j, b, j, h, d, h, d, h, c, j, c, e, a, e, j, 3xd, j, c, j, i, c, i, c, f, c, j, d, j, i, d, i, d, j, 3xe, j, f, j, a, j, 5xe, j, f, j, d, j, d, j, d, j, 3xe, b, j, a, j, b, h, d, h, d, h, d, 2xe, j, e, f, e, j, c, e, d, j, d, j, d, e, c, e, c, 3xe, c, j, h, a, j, 3xe, b, e, j, a, j, e, 3xh, c, h, c, e, d, j, 3xd, j, 2xe, j, a, j, a, j, h, c, j, 3xe, c, e, j, f, e, j, e, j, e, c, e, j, crimp
    Long strand pattern—crimp, j, b, j, e, d, 2xe, c, I, c, I, c, 3xh, 2xe, j, a, j, b, e, f, e, c, h, c, j, b, j, h, j, b, j, h, j b, e, a, j, e, d, e, d, e, d, h, d, h, c, j, a, j, e, f, e, b, e, d, h, d, h, c, e, c, e, c, j, e, f, e, j, b, e, a, j, silver disc bead, j, a, j, a, j, a, j, e, f, e, j, 2xe, f, e, j, d, h, d, h, d, j, e, f, e, c, e, b, e, b, e, j, h, d, I, c, I, c, j, 5xe, j, I, d, I, d, I, d, I, j, e, f, e, j, e, c, e, c, e, c, j, b, j, a, j, 3xe, j, c, I, d, I, d, b, e, crimp

TOOLS
Wire Cutters, Crimping Pliers

MATERIALS:
16	7mm to 10mm frosted glass spiral beads (a)
17	7mm x 2.5mm frosted glass long rice-shaped beads (b)
31	4mm round frosted glass beads (c)
42	4mm to 6mm rondel frosted glass beads (d)
100	size 11/0 seed beads (e)
12	4mm x 5mm Thai silver box-shape decorated beads (f)
1	10mm Thai silver decorated disc bead (g)
30	4mm Thai silver daisy spacer beds (h)
16	3mm silver torus shape spacer beds (i)
66	2mm silver hollow round beads (j)
1	20mm silver puzzle clasp
4	silver crimp beads
4	silver bead covers
40"	of gold color beading wire

NOTE
As with any designs that have randomly arranged appearances, I urge you to vary the colors and patterns to suit your own taste. In this design, make sure that the silver disc bead is in the center of the longer strand. Hold the strands up periodically as you string to make sure that there is a pleasing balance of beads.

BOHEMIAN LAMPWORK GLASS NECKLACE

CZECH DESIGNER ALENA CHLADKOVA HAS ADDED A COMPLETELY NEW DIMENSION TO THE TRADITIONAL BOHEMIAN GLASS BEAD INDUSTRY. HER LAMPWORK BEADS ARE FILLED WITH YOUTHFUL VITALITY AND JOY, EXPLORING EXCITING COLOR COMBINATIONS AND PATTERNS. THIS LONG ROPE NECKLACE, COMPOSED ALMOST ENTIRELY OF CHLADKOVA'S BEADS, DISPLAYS THE BREADTH OF HER TALENT.

1. Thread a crimp onto the beading wire. Pass the beading wire through the ring of one half of the clasp and then back through the crimp. Make sure that the beading wire is tight around the ring. Squeeze the crimp shut. Thread on a 3mm and a 2mm silver bead.

2. There are two ways to approach this kind of seemingly random design: You can lay all the beads out on a bead board or on a soft surface and arrange them before stringing, or you can simply start putting beads on the wire and keep reviewing as you go to make sure there is some sense of balance to the design. A rope of this length can certainly motivate you to use the latter method. Do not get too anxious about the order of the beads—you can always take them off and start over again if it is not coming together as you wish. Inspect the strand every 4" or so to see if it is to your liking.

3. End with a 2mm bead, a 3mm gold bead, and a crimp. Bring the beading wire through the ring of the other side of the clasp and then back through the crimp and the round bead. Tighten the necklace so there are no spaces between the beads, close the crimp, and snip off any remaining beading wire. Add the crimp covers.

THIS NECKLACE IS A PERFECT EXAMPLE OF WHY GLASS BEADS ARE SO APPEALING TO THE JEWELRY MAKER—NO OTHER MEDIUM OFFERS THE POSSIBILITY OF SO MUCH VARIETY AND INNOVATION. TO GIVE EACH ONE OF THESE LOVELY BEADS SPACE TO SHOW OFF, I HAVE USED LONG SILVER TUBES AS SPACERS.

TOOLS
Wire Cutters, Crimping Pliers

MATERIALS (TO MAKE A 68" ROPE)

56	assorted lampwork glass beads
51	Swarovski crystal bicone beads from 3mm to 6mm
48	7mm x 1mm silver tubes
17	3mm x 6mm silver decorated rondel beads
2	3mm double daisy silver spacer beads
13	4.5mm fluted silver bead caps
3	8mm square silver beads
5	7mm x 11mm silver bell charms
226	3mm or 2mm silver hollow seamless round beads
1	19mm silver toggle clasp
2	silver crimp beads
2	silver bead covers
6"	of beading wire

NOTE
To make the glass beads sit well on the wire, use a 3mm round silver bead at each end. If the glass bead is round, use a silver bead cap. Be sure to place a 2mm bead at each end of the tubes to give a pleasing visual effect and help transition to the next bead. This also prevents the silver tubes from entering the hole of the adjacent bead and making the necklace less flexible.

METAL SEED BEADS WITH LAMPWORK CENTERPIECE NECKLACE

THIS BEAUTIFUL LAMPWORK CENTERPIECE BEAD BY CYNTHIA SAARI IS SPECKLED WITH METALLIC INCLUSIONS. TO MATCH ITS EARTHY LOOK, I HAVE USED MULTIPLE STRANDS OF TINY HANDMADE METAL BEADS SPRINKLED WITH METALLIC SHEEN GLASS SEED BEADS. IF YOU CAN'T FIND THESE AFRICAN METAL BEADS, USE GOLD- AND SILVER-PLATED CHARLOTTES INSTEAD.

1. Start by wire-wrapping the centerpiece bead. Grip about ⅛" at the end of the 18 gauge silver wire with your flat-nosed pliers and then squeeze tightly until the end is flattened. Add a 5mm silver disc bead, the lampwork bead, and another 5mm disc to the wire. Cut the wire about ¾" above the last bead and make a wire-wrapped loop. (Tip: If the hole of a lampwork glass bead is large and makes the bead move around on the wire, add small seed beads to the wire first; this will thicken the wire and fill the hole more tightly.)

2. Cut the beading wire into five pieces, each about 28" long. Put transparent tape around one end of one of the pieces of the beading wire to keep the beads from falling off (or use a tight bead stopper). Make a strand of brass beads interspersed with cylinder beads, each 23" long (or the length you prefer). The pattern is quite random, so you can use your own judgment about how to mix them, or you can refer to the photograph for guidance. Pass this strand through one of the large-hole silver beads, the loop of the centerpiece, and the other large-hole silver bead. Tape the other end of the strand so that the beads cannot fall off.

   Make two more strands in the same manner. Make sure that the beaded strands are even in length and that the centerpiece and its bracketing silver beads are at the center of the strands.

TOOLS
Wire Cutters, Crimping Pliers, Flat-Nosed Pliers

MATERIALS

- 1   large lampwork centerpiece bead
- 1½   34" strands of African handmade brass seed beads
- 1½   34" strands of African handmade silver-colored seed beads
- 1½   grams of size 11/0 purple iris cylinder beads (these are Miyuki Delicas)
- 1   gram of size 11/0 blue iris cylinder beads (these are Miyuki Delicas)
- 2   4mm silver disc beads
- 2   5mm brushed silver round beads with large holes
- 2   3mm hollow seamless silver round beads
- 1   13mm gold filled lobster clasp
- 2   12mm vermeil cones
- 1   6mm gold-filled soldered ring
- 1   4mm gold-filled jump ring
- 3"   of 18 gauge silver wire
- 4"   of 22 gauge silver wire
- 12'   of beading wire

3. Pass the fourth piece of beading wire through both the large-hole silver beads and the loop of the centerpiece. Make sure the ends are even with the strands you have already beaded. Now, add a mixture of silvery metallic beads and cylinder beads to each side of the beading wire until the beaded parts match the brass bead strands in length. Tape both ends of the strand to keep the beads from falling off. Repeat this step with the final piece of beading wire.

4. Cut the 22 gauge wire into two 2" pieces. Make a wire-wrapped loop at one end of one piece. Remove the tape from one end of a beaded strand. Add a crimp to the strand, and bring the beading wire through the loop of the silver wire and then back through the crimp. Before you squeeze the crimp shut, it is very important that you adjust the wires so the beads are all snug, with no gaps between them. Repeat this procedure with the other four strands so one side of the strand cluster is attached to the loop of the silver wire. Then make a wire-wrapped loop at the end of the other piece of silver wire, and repeat the above with the other side of the necklace strands.

5. Add a cone to one of the pieces of silver wire so it fits over the loop and the ends of the strands. Add a 3mm silver bead on the wire at the top of the cone. Make sure that the cone sits firmly against the strands. Cut the wire about $^3/_8$" from the silver beads. Make the beginnings of a wire-wrapped loop. Pass it through the ring of the lobster clasp and finish wrapping to secure it. Repeat this step to finish the other side of the necklace, but use a jump ring to attach the wire-wrapped loop to a 6mm soldered ring.

NOTE

The key to this necklace is to get all five strands clustered at a central point. How you do this depends on the size of the holes of the two silver centering beads. My beads had holes large enough to fit three filled strands; I have given the directions accordingly. If your beads have smaller holes, start with just one or two filled strands and then pass through the empty wire before completing.

GLASS AND SILVER-PLATED NECKLACE

THESE SOFT-HUED GLASS BEADS ARE MADE OF BOROSILICATE GLASS, SOMETIMES KNOWN AS PYREX. THE HARDNESS AND CLARITY OF THIS TYPE OF GLASS GIVE A PARTICULAR REFLECTIVE QUALITY, WHILE THE COLOR RANGE OFFERS SOME VERY SUBTLE ORGANIC TONES. THE LOVELY BLUE-BROWN SHADES OF THESE BEADS MATCH PERFECTLY WITH SILVER. ALTHOUGH THE BEADS ARE HANDMADE INDIVIDUALLY, THEY ARE INEXPENSIVE AND CAN BE MATCHED WITH GOOD-QUALITY SILVER PLATE. IN THIS CASE, THE GLASS BEADS ARE MATCHED WITH BEADS AND FINDINGS FROM TIERRACAST, AN AMERICAN BEAD MANUFACTURER. BECAUSE THE NECKLACE IS LONG ENOUGH TO FIT OVER THE HEAD, IT DOES NOT NEED A CLASP.

1. Cut 1¼" of the silver wire. Use your round-nosed pliers to make a simple loop at one end of the cut piece. Now add a round silver bead, a bead cap, a glass bead, another bead cap, and another round bead. Make a simple loop the same size as the first one. Make sure that beads are snug between the two loops. If they are not, then the wire is a bit too long. Open the loop and cut the wire a bit shorter so when the loop is made, the end of it sits firmly against the last bead.

2. Cut the rest of the wire into 1¼" pieces (or shorter, if the first was too long). Use all of the glass and round beads, as well as the bead caps, to make another twenty-six pieces in the same way as above.

3. Open a jump ring and slip it onto a square. Add the loop of a glass bead piece to the same jump ring and close. Add an open jump ring to the other loop of the glass piece and then another glass piece to the same jump ring and close. Add an open jump ring to the other loop of that glass piece and then another glass piece to the same jump ring and close. Now, use another jump ring to attach the other loop to a square. Repeat this pattern of one square to three glass pieces until you have used all the components. Finally, attach the last jump ring to the square with which you started.

TOOLS
Wire Cutters, Round-Nosed Pliers

MATERIALS (FOR A 26" NECKLACE)

27	8mm borosilicate lampwork glass rondel beads
54	6mm silver-plated bead caps
2	2.5mm silver hollow seamless round beads
9	11mm silver-plated squares
36	6mm silver jump rings
27"	of 20 gauge silver wire

GLASS THAT GLITTERS LIKE GOLD NECKLACE

SOME GLASS BEADS ARE SO SENSATIONAL THAT SOLID GOLD IS THEIR NATURAL PARTNER. THESE BEAUTIFUL BEADS ARE MADE BY AMERICAN GLASS BEAD ARTIST SCOTT TURNBULL. HIS SPECIALTY IS USING THE IRIDESCENT QUALITIES OF DICHROIC GLASS. HERE HE HAS COMBINED IT WITH 23-KARAT GOLD LEAF TO CREATE AN EFFECT RICH ENOUGH TO BE COMPLEMENTED BY THE GOLD OF THE HOLLOW CUBE BEADS.

1. Start the necklace by threading on a crimp. Pass the beading wire through the ring of one half of the clasp and then back through the crimp. Make sure that the beading wire is tight around the ring. Squeeze the crimp shut. Add a 2.5mm gold round bead to cover the tail of the beading wire and cut.

2. Now thread on a gold cube bead, a 1.5mm round bead, a dichroic glass bead, and another 1.5mm round bead. Repeat this pattern twenty-two times or until the necklace is the length you wish. (Remember to try the necklace on to make sure you've reached the right length.)

3. Add a final gold cube bead, a 2.5mm round bead, and a crimp. Bring the beading wire through the ring of the other side of the clasp and then back through the crimp and round bead. Now, tighten the necklace so there are no spaces between the beads, close the crimp, and snip off any remaining beading wire. Add the crimp covers to the crimps.

TOOLS
Wire Cutters, Crimping Pliers

MATERIALS

23	13mm dichroic glass round beads with interior gold
24	5mm 18 karat gold hollow cube beads.
2	2.5mm 18 karat gold-filled hollow seamless round beads
46	2mm 18 karat gold-filled hollow seamless round beads
2	gold-filled crimp beads
2	gold-filled crimp covers
1	18-karat gold toggle clasp
20"	of beading wire

NOTE
Sometimes the holes of lampwork glass beads are so large that they do not sit snugly on the beading wire but move around in an unattractive way. The solution is to use tiny round beads that fit into the holes of the lampwork beads. I have used that solution in this necklace. The 2mm beads are hardly seen, as they are covered by the holes of the glass beads, but they are essential to making the necklace work properly. If you were using glass beads with smaller holes, they would not be necessary. If the holes are so large that the little gold beads do not hold them properly, put some seed beads on the wire between the gold beads so the dichroic beads fit over them and are kept from moving around.

OPAQUE LAMPWORK GLASS NECKLACE

I LOVE THE NATURAL, EARTHY LOOK OF THESE CHINESE
LAMPWORK BEADS. WHILE THEY AREN'T MEANT TO IMITATE
GEMSTONES, THEY DO HAVE A JASPER-LIKE APPEARANCE. I HAVE
USED GREEN GARNETS AS SPACER BEADS TO ACCENTUATE THE
NATURAL STONE LOOK, AS WELL AS A VERMEIL CENTER BEAD TO
BRING THE BROWN AND GREEN HUES TOGETHER.

1. Thread a crimp onto the beading wire. Pass the beading wire
   through the ring of one half of the clasp and then back through
   the crimp. Make sure that the beading wire is tight around the
   ring. Squeeze the crimp shut. Thread on a 3mm gold bead and
   two 4mm garnet beads.

2. Add a 4mm garnet bead , a glass rondel, G, R, G, R, G, R, G, R, G,
   a 6mm garnet bead, R, G, R, G, R, G, R, G, R, G, and a large oval
   glass bead. Repeat this pattern three times.

3. Add a 4mm bead, a rondel, and a 6mm bead; then, add the large
   gold center bead, a 6mm bead, a rondel, and a 4mm bead.

4. Now, reverse the original pattern (starting with the large oval
   glass bead and ending with a 4mm garnet bead) and repeat it
   four times. Add two more 4mm garnets, a 3mm gold bead, and a
   crimp. Bring the beading wire through the ring of the other side
   of the clasp and then back through the crimp and round bead.
   Now, tighten the necklace so there are no spaces between the
   beads, close the crimp, and snip off any remaining beading
   wire. Add the crimp covers.

TOOLS
Wire Cutters, Crimping Pliers

MATERIALS (TO MAKE A 26" NECKLACE)
- 8 20mm x 25mm flat oval lampwork glass beads
- 82 9mm rondel lampwork glass beads (R)
- 10 6mm round green garnet beads
- 86 4mm round green garnet beads (G)
- 1 11mm x 15mm vermeil bead
- 2 3mm gold-filled hollow seamless round beads
- 1 15mm vermeil toggle clasp
- 2 gold-filled crimp beads
- 2 gold-filled bead covers
- 28" of gold color beading wire

DICHROIC GLASS BRACELET

DICHROIC GLASS BEADS CAN BE EXPENSIVE, BUT JUST A DOZEN OR SO CAN MAKE A MEMORABLE BRACELET. WHILE NEARLY ALL OF THESE BEADS DIFFER IN SHAPE OR PATTERN, THEY ARE NONETHELESS UNITED BY THEIR RED TONES (RED CALLS FOR GOLD). IN THIS CASE, I USED A MORE ECONOMICAL VERMEIL. THIS KIND OF RANDOM DESIGN IS GREAT FOR USING UP LEFTOVER BEADS FROM OTHER PROJECTS.

1. First, make the dangle which will hang on the clasp. Onto the headpin add a 3mm gold bead, a dichroic glass bead, and another 3mm gold bead. Use the round-nosed pliers to begin a wire-wrapped loop with the rest of the headpin. Slip the loop over the ring of the circular part of the toggle clasp and close it by wire wrapping.

2. Thread a crimp onto the beading wire. Pass the beading wire through the ring of the same half of the clasp and then back through the crimp. Make sure the beading wire is tight around the ring. Squeeze the crimp shut. Thread on a 3mm gold bead and a small dichroic bead. Continue to add combinations of dichroic and gold until they are all on the wire. Use the 3mm gold beads as spacers against the large holes of the dichroic beads. This will prevent the beads from sitting loosely on the beading wire.

3. Now, hold the bracelet around your wrist to see if you like how the beads are arranged. Until you are familiar with making this kind of seemingly random selection, it is unlikely that the first arrangement will be the one you want. Luckily, the beads should be easy to remove and rearrange.

4. When the design pleases you and the bracelet fits well, add a 3mm gold bead and a crimp. Bring the beading wire through the ring of the other side of the clasp and then back through the crimp and round bead. Tighten the bracelet so there are no spaces between the beads, close the crimp, and snip off any remaining beading wire. Add the crimp covers.

TOOLS

Wire Cutters, Crimping Pliers, Round-Nosed Pliers

MATERIALS (FOR A 7" BRACELET)

12 dichroic glass beads from 5mm round to 18mm x 10mm barrel

10 assorted vermeil beads and spacers from 6mm to 12mm

18 3mm gold-filled hollow seamless round beads

1 13mm vermeil toggle clasp

2 gold-filled crimp beads

2 gold-filled crimp bead covers

1 1" gold-filled headpin with ball end

10" of beading wire

THREE-IN-ONE PRESSED GLASS AND SILVER NECKLACE

EACH OF THE THREE STRANDS OF THIS NECKLACE IS FINISHED AT BOTH ENDS WITH A SPRING RING CLASP SO THEY CAN BE WORN AS INDIVIDUAL NECKLACES OR USED AN EYEGLASS LEASH.

As with all designs that have a randomly arranged appearance, I would urge you to vary the colors and patterns to suit both your personal taste and the availability of the beads. If you want to follow my design exactly, use the following patterns, which are based on the code in the materials list.

1. For strand 1: Use the silver wire to wire wrap the following combinations: 3x (H, E, H); 3x (H, F, BF, H); 2x (H, A, A, A, H); 1x (H, D, G, B, G, D, H); 2x (H, C, H); 1x (H, A, A, A, A, A, A, H); 2x (H, G, D, D, D, G, H); 1x (H, B, H); 1x (H, G, D, G, H). Cut the silver chain into ten 1" pieces and seven ½" pieces. Use the jump rings to join the pieces of chain to the wire-wrapped pieces so that every wire-wrapped piece is separated by chain. Attach the spring ring clasps to the ends of the chain using two more jump rings. Make six dangles with the headpins and remaining rondels (D), and then attach them at random to several jump rings.

2. For strand 2: Thread a crimp onto the beading wire; pass the wire through the loop of the clasp and then back through the crimp. Squeeze the crimp shut. Thread on a 2.5mm silver bead (H). Now add 28 charlotte beads (J), a bead cap (F), an 8mm (B), and another bead cap (F). Repeat this pattern 16 more times and then add a final group of 28 charlotte beads. Add a 3mm silver bead and a crimp; attach to the other side of the clasp.

TOOLS
Wire Cutters, Crimping Pliers

MATERIALS
Strand 1

11	10mm pressed glass leaf-shaped beads (A)
6	8mm round pressed glass beads (B)
3	7mm x 8mm fire-polished faceted pressed glass bead (F)
13	4mm x 6mm facetted rondel pressed glass beads (D)
3	6mm silver decorated rondel beads (D)
6	7mm silver decorated bead caps (F)
12	4mm silver daisy spacer beds (G)
39	2.5mm silver hollow round beads (H)
6½"	headpins with ball tips
34	4mm silver jump rings
2	6mm silver spring ring clasps
30"	of 26 gauge silver wire
16"	of silver chain with 3mm links

Strand 2

17	8mm round pressed glass beads (B)
2	12" strands of size 13/0 charlotte seed beads (J)
34	7mm silver decorated bead caps (F)
2	2.5mm silver hollow round beads (H)
2	6mm silver spring ring clasps
2	silver crimp beads
2	silver bead covers
34"	of beading wire

3. For strand 3: Thread a crimp onto the beading wire; pass the wire through the loop of the clasp and then back through the crimp; squeeze the crimp shut. Thread on the following: S, 7J, B, 7J, S, 3A, S, 7J, S, K, S, 3J, S, B, S, 3J, S, K, S, 7J, S, 5A, S, 3J, B, 3J, S, D, S, 5J, H, E, H, 5J, S, J, S, K, S, J, S, K, S, J, S, K, S, J, S, C, S, 5J, S, J, B, J, S, 5J, S, D, S, D, S, D, S, 7J, S, 3A, S, 7J, S, J, S, K, S, J, S, B, S, J, S, K, S, J, S, 7J, S, 5A, S, 5J, H, E, H, 5J, S, J, B, J, S, 5J, S, 3A, S, 5J, S, K, S, J, S, 5J, S, C, S, J, S, K, S, J, S, 7J, S, B, S, J, S, B, S, J, S, B, S, 7J, S, D, S, 3J, S, H, E, H, 9A. Now, using the last set of leaf-shaped beads as the center point, reverse the pattern to copy it so the other side of the necklace matches the first. Add a crimp, and attach the strand to the final spring ring clasp. Hook all of the spring ring clasps onto the 8mm silver ring to create the three-strand necklace.

Strand 3

47	10mm pressed glass leaf-shaped beads (A)
18	8mm round pressed glass beads (B)
18	4mm flat faceted disc pressed glass beads (K)
13	4mm x 6mm facetted rondel pressed glass beads (D)
4	7mm x 8mm fire-polished faceted pressed glass bead (C)
6	6mm silver decorated rondel beads (E)
1	12" strand of size 13/0 charlotte seed beads (J)
125	size 13/0 silver plated charlotte seed beads (S)
12	2.5mm silver hollow round beads (H)
2	6mm silver spring ring clasps
2	silver crimp beads
2	silver bead covers
36"	of beading wire

To connect all: an 8mm silver spring ring

SILVER AND GLASS EARRINGS ENCORE

IN THIS DESIGN, THE SILVER FLATTERS THE GLASS BEAD. YOU CAN ALMOST HEAR IT SAYING, "LOOK AT ME—I'M NOT JUST A SIMPLE BIT OF GLASS, BUT RATHER A BEAD TO BE TAKEN SERIOUSLY." ANY BEAD THAT CAN WEAR SUCH A LARGE SOLID SILVER BEAD CAP COMMANDS RESPECT. ANY BEAD YOU FIND PARTICULARLY BEAUTIFUL COULD STAND THE SAME TREATMENT.

1. Add a round silver bead, a silver disc, and a glass bead to a headpin. Now, add the silver cap so it fits over the glass bead. Add one more round silver bead.

2. Cut the headpin so about 1/2" is left above the last bead. Make a wire-wrapped loop. Attach it to the earwire by opening the loop at the bottom of the earwire.

TOOLS
Round-Nosed Pliers, Flat-Nosed Pliers, Wire Cutters

MATERIALS:
- 2 13mm round lampwork glass beads
- 2 9mm x 15mm decorated silver bead caps
- 2 3.5mm flat disc silver spacer beads
- 4 3mm seamless hollow silver round beads
- 2 1 1/2" silver headpins with ball tip
- 2 silver earwires with decoration

LAMPWORK GLASS AND SILVER DISCS EARRINGS

THESE LAMPWORK BEADS ARE SIMPLE, BUT THE DEEP RED CORE WRAPPED WITH AMBER GLASS GIVES THEM A RICH APPEARANCE WHICH HELPS CREATE THE RIGHT BALANCE WITH THE LARGER SILVER DISCS. THE PERFORATED NATURE OF THE DISCS GIVING THEM A LIGHT AND AIRY LOOK THAT ALLOWS THE BEADS TO PLAY AN EQUAL ROLE.

1. To an eyepin add a round silver bead, a glass bead, and one more round silver bead.

2. Cut the headpin about 1/4" above the last bead and make a simple loop. Attach it to the earwire by opening the loop at the bottom of the earwire.

3. Open the loop at the bottom of the eyepin and add the silver disc.

TOOLS
Round-Nosed Pliers, Flat-Nosed Pliers, Wire Cutters

MATERIALS
- 2 11mm round lampwork glass beads
- 2 18mm silver disc pendants
- 4 3mm seamless hollow silver round beads
- 2 1 1/2" silver eyepins
- 2 silver earwires

SILVER WITH A GLASS "HAT" EARRINGS

THE PRESSED GLASS BEAD CAPS USED HERE TURN THE TABLES ON THE TRADITIONAL GOLD OR SILVER BEAD CAP AND MAKE FOR AN INTRIGUING DESIGN.

1. Add a 2mm round silver bead, a round glass bead, and another 2mm silver bead to a 1" headpin. Cut the headpin leaving about $\frac{1}{4}$" to make a simple loop.

2. Put a $\frac{1}{2}$" headpin through one of the holes in the silver ribs bead so the ball tip is inside the ribs of the bead. Cut the headpin leaving about $\frac{1}{4}$" to make a simple loop. Use this loop to attach to the loop with the round glass bead.

3. Pass a 1" headpin with a ball tip through the other hole in the silver ribs bead as you did in Step 2. Add a glass bead cap so the concave side faces the silver ribs bead. Add a 3mm and a 2.5mm silver bead. Cut the headpin leaving $\frac{5}{8}$" and make a wire-wrapped loop. Attach the earwire to the wire-wrapped loop.

TOOLS
Round-Nosed Pliers, Flat-Nosed Pliers, Wire Cutters

MATERIALS
- 2 22mm pressed glass bead caps
- 2 10mm round pressed glass beads
- 2 14mm silver rib beads comprising 2 silver circles set at right angles to each other
- 2 3mm seamless hollow silver round beads
- 2 2.5mm hollow silver round beads
- 4 2mm hollow silver round beads
- 2 1" silver headpins
- 2 $\frac{1}{2}$" silver headpins with ball tip
- 2 1" silver headpins with ball tip
- 2 silver earwires

CRYSTAL BARBELL AND SILVER CHAIN EARRINGS

THIS NEW SHAPE FROM SWAROVSKI IS LIKE A TINY FACETED BARBELL. THE "ADD-ON" EARWIRES ALLOW FOR EASY EMBELLISHMENT.

1. Add three crystal beads and a 3mm silver bead to a 1" headpin. Make sure the crystal beads are tightly seated on each other. Start a wire-wrapped loop, but before wrapping, hook on to it one of the pieces of chain.

2. Add a 2mm silver bead, a crystal bead, and another 2mm bead to the "add-on" earwire; make a simple loop. Open the loop, attach it to the other end of the chain, and close.

TOOLS
Round-Nosed Pliers, Flat-Nosed Pliers, Wire Cutters

MATERIALS
- 8 11mm x 5mm Swarovski "barbell" crystal beads
- 2 3mm seamless hollow silver round beads
- 4 2mm hollow silver round beads
- 2 1" silver headpins with ball tip
- 2 1" pieces of silver cable chain with 3.5mm links
- 2 silver "add-on" earwires

DICHROIC GLASS EARRINGS

WHEN THE GLASS IS AS STUNNING AS THESE DICHROIC SQUARES BY SCOTT TURNBALL, IT REQUIRES ONLY THE SIMPLEST OF SETTINGS TO BECOME DAZZLING EARRINGS. HERE THE JET BLACK ONYX BEADS MATCH THE UNDERLYING COLOR OF THE MAIN BEAD.

1. Add a gold-filled bead, a dichroic bead, another gold-filled bead, a black onyx bead, and another gold-filled bead to a headpin. Cut the headpin at least $1/4$" above the round bead, and make a simple loop.

2. Slip the loop onto the loop of the earwire and close.

TOOLS
Round-Nosed Pliers, Flat-Nosed Pliers, Wire Cutters

MATERIALS
- 2 11mm flat square dichroic glass beads
- 2 4mm faceted round black onyx beads
- 6 3mm gold-filled seamless hollow round beads
- 2 $1^{1}/_{2}$" gold-filled headpins with ball tip
- 2 gold-filled earwires

DICHROIC GLASS WITH GOLD AND PERIDOT EARRINGS

AN UNDERLYING CORE OF GREEN GLASS FLASHES THROUGH
THE BRIGHT BRONZE OF THE DICHROIC FIRE IN THESE BEADS
INSPIRED BY THE ADDITION OF PALE GREEN PERIDOT DANGLES.

1. Add a faceted bead, a dichroic bead, another faceted bead, a peridot bead, and a final faceted bead to a 1" headpin. Make a simple loop.

2. Add a faceted bead, a peridot bead, a daisy spacer bead, another peridot bead, and a faceted bead to another 1" headpin. Cut the headpin leaving ¼" and make a simple loop.

3. Add a faceted bead, three daisy spacer beads, and another faceted bead to a third 1" headpin. Cut the headpin leaving ¼" and make a simple loop.

4. Open a jump ring. Pass it through the loops of the three headpins, the loop of the earwire, and close.

TOOLS
Round-Nosed Pliers, Flat-Nosed Pliers,
Wire Cutters

MATERIALS
- 2　10mm rondel dichroic glass beads
- 6　3.5mm round peridot beads
- 8　4mm vermeil daisy spacer beads
- 14　2.1mm gold-filled hollow faceted beads
- 6　1" gold-filled headpins
- 2　3.5mm gold-filled jump rings
- 2　vermeil decorated earwires

GLASS AND SILVER ROPE NECKLACE

ASIDE FROM THE SILVER AND A FEW TINY CRYSTALS, THE BEADS IN THIS NECKLACE ARE INEXPENSIVE PRESSED GLASS. SOME OF THE BEADS HAVE AN AB COATING, WHICH GIVES AN OILY IRIDESCENCE TO THE SURFACE. OTHERS ARE FIRE-POLISHED, A TECHNIQUE THAT CREATES A PARTICULARLY SMOOTH, SLICK EXTERIOR APPEARANCE. BOTH METHODS OF FINISHING PRESSED GLASS CREATE A REFLECTIVE SURFACE THAT GOES VERY WELL WITH SILVER'S NATURAL SHINE. A LONG ROPE OF THIS KIND CAN BE WOUND AROUND THE NECK MORE THAN ONCE.

1. Thread a crimp onto the beading wire; pass the wire through a jump ring and back through the crimp. Then use the photo on page 114 and the following rules to add your beads:

   a) Every silver tube should have a 2mm round silver bead at each end.

   b) Every pressed glass bead and large Bali-style silver bead should have a small silver spacer bead or 2mm crystal bead at each end.

   c) The leaf beads should be used in clusters of three or five.

   d) Use the large silver beads and the baroque glass beads individually.

   e) Use all the other glass beads individually or in groups of three.

2. When you reach the end of your supply of beads, or when the necklace is long enough, add a final 3mm round silver bead and a bead crimp. Attach the wire to the other side of the clasp, making sure all the beads are tight against one another before closing the crimp. Snip off any remaining wire and add the crimp covers.

TOOLS
Wire Cutters, Crimping Pliers

MATERIALS (TO MAKE AN 80" ROPE NECKLACE)

165   assorted pressed glass beads, either AB coated or fire-polished, including forty-three leaf shapes; seven 10mm baroque shapes; two 15mm butterflies; and a variety of 4mm to 11mm round, cube, rondel, and teardrop shapes

18   2mm round Swarovski crystal beads

8   6mm x 8mm Bali-style silver beads

94   4mm daisy silver spacer beads

22   4mm daisy silver spacer beads

33   12mm x 1mm silver spacer tubes

24   6mm x 1mm silver spacer tubes

130   assorted 3mm and 2mm silver hollow round spacer beads

1   7mm x 17mm hook and eye clasp

2   silver crimp beads

2   silver crimp bead covers

84"   of beading wire

NOTE
This kind of random design is easier to do if you create it right on the wire rather than lay all the beads out before you string. You must review it every six inches or so to make sure there is some sense of balance to the design. Do not get too anxious about the order of the beads—you can always take them off and start over if the piece is not coming out how you envisioned.

SILVER FOIL LAMPWORK GLASS NECKLACE

ALTHOUGH EACH SIDE OF THIS NECKLACE IS NOT A MIRROR IMAGE OF THE OTHER, THE NECKLACE IS NOT ASYMMETRICAL. ENSURE THAT THE SILVER CENTER BEAD ENDS UP IN THE CENTER AND THAT THE SIX SYMMETRICAL "MARKER BEADS" FALL OPPOSITE THEIR TWINS.

1. Thread a crimp onto the beading wire; pass the last ring of one half of the clasp back through the crimp. Make sure that the beading wire is tight around the ring. Squeeze the crimp shut. Thread on a 3mm silver bead (sb), a 4mm daisy bead (d), a 7mm turquoise bead, d, a seed pearl, a facetted gemstone bead (fg), sb, a dichroic bead, sb, a Bali-style bead, sb, a two-tone glass bead, a 7mm daisy bead, sb, a 10mm silver bead (marker bead #1), sb, fg, d, a turquoise bead, d, fg, d, sb, a silver foil lamp glass bead (marker bead #2), d, fg, sb, a 7mm daisy bead, sb, a silver foil glass bead, sb, a seed pearl, d, sb, d, fg, d4, sb, a silver foil glass bead (marker bead #3), sb, a silver foil glass bead, sb, and a large, flat silver oval bead.

2. Remember to keep holding the necklace up to compare the positions of the six marker beads (two pairs of glass beads and one pair of silver beads) which will give a sense of symmetry to the design. Add sb, d, d, d, sb, and the glass bead that pairs with marker bead #3.

3. Continue by adding sb, a seed pearl, d, fg, sb, a silver foil glass bead, sb, a 10mm silver bead, sb, fg, d, sb, and the twin of marker bead #2. Hold the necklace to check that the large flat silver bead is centered between marker #2 and its twin. Add or subtract a bead or two between this bead and the previous marker bead so that marker #2 will end up as its twin.

4. Continue adding sb, d, fg, d, fg, d, fg, d, sb, and a 10mm silver bead. This should fall opposite marker bead #1. Hold up the necklace and, if necessary, adjust as you did previously; then, add sb, d, a turquoise bead, d, sb, a silver foil glass bead, sb, a silver foil glass bead, sb, d, fg, d, sb, and a crimp. Bring the beading wire through the last ring of the other side of the clasp and then back through the crimp and round bead. Now tighten the necklace, close the crimp, and snip off any remaining beading wire. Add the crimp covers.

TOOLS
Wire Cutters, Crimping Pliers

MATERIALS

11	assorted lampwork glass with silver foil beads, including 2 pairs of the same style, shape, and size (the glass marker beads)
11	assorted faceted gemstone beads from 3mm to 7mm (fg)
3	8mm round turquoise beads
3	white seed pearls
11	10mm round decorated silver beads
1	7mm Bali-style silver bead
2	7mm daisy silver spacer beads
22	4mm daisy silver spacer beads (d)
1	19mm x 23mm decorated flat oval Thai silver bead
28	3mm silver hollow seamless round beads (sb)
1	12mm silver toggle clasp with chain extender
2	silver crimp beads
2	silver crimp bead covers
20"	of beading wire

CRYSTAL PEARL EARRINGS

GLASS HAS LONG BEEN USED TO CREATE IMITATION PEARLS. FOR AT LEAST THREE CENTURIES, THE ART OF COATING THE INSIDES OF HOLLOW GLASS BEADS WITH A SOLUTION OF FISH SCALES PROVIDED A CLOSE FACSIMILE OF THE REAL THING. MODERN TECHNOLOGY HAS PRODUCED COATINGS AND COATING METHODS THAT CAN PRODUCE A PEARL-LIKE LUSTER ON THE OUTSIDES OF BEADS STRONG ENOUGH TO STAND UP TO FREQUENT WEAR.

1. Add a 4mm crystal pearl, a silver rondel, an 8mm crystal pearl, another rondel, a 12mm crystal pearl, and a 2mm silver round bead to a headpin.

2. Cut the headpin at least ¼" above the round bead; make a simple loop. Slip the loop onto the loop of the earwire and close.

TOOLS
Round-Nosed Pliers, Flat-Nosed Pliers, Wire Cutters

MATERIALS
- 2   12mm Swarovski crystal pearls
- 2   8mm Swarovski crystal pearls
- 2   4mm Swarovski crystal pearls
- 2   6mm silver-plated rondel spacer beads
- 2   2mm seamless hollow silver round beads
- 2   1½" silver headpins with ball tip
- 2   silver earwires

LAMPWORK EARRINGS

THE SAME SHAPE IN SEVERAL COLORS, OR THE SAME DESIGN IN SEVERAL SHAPES, GIVES THE JEWELRY DESIGNER A FAR GREATER SCOPE FOR HIS OR HER OWN DESIGNS. THESE EARRINGS DEMONSTRATE HOW USEFUL IT IS TO HAVE BOTH A ROUND VERSION AND A RECTANGULAR ONE OF THE SAME BEAD DESIGN.

1. Add a 2.5mm silver bead, a large rectangular lampwork bead, another 2.5mm silver bead, a 9mm round glass bead, and another 2.5mm silver bead to a headpin.

2. Cut the headpin at least ¼" above the round bead; make a simple loop. Slip the loop onto the loop of the earwire and then close.

TOOLS
Round-Nosed Pliers, Flat-Nosed Pliers, Wire Cutters

MATERIALS
- 2   13mm x 15mm rectangular lampwork glass beads
- 2   9mm round lampwork glass beads
- 6   2.5mm hollow silver round beads
- 2   2" silver headpins with ball tip
- 2   silver earwires

FUMED LAMPWORK GLASS EARRINGS

LAMPWORK BEADMAKERS CAN APPLY PRECIOUS METAL TO THEIR CREATIONS WITH VERY THIN METAL LEAF OR THROUGH A DELICATE PROCESS CALLED FUMING. THIS METHOD INVOLVES HEATING A TINY SPECK OF GOLD OR SILVER AT THE BASE OF A FLAME. AS THE METAL MELTS, A SMALL AMOUNT OF IT FORMS A FUME, OR SMOKE. AS THE FUME TOUCHES THE HOT BEAD, IT BONDS TO THE GLASS, FORMING A THIN FILM OF PRECIOUS METAL ON THE SURFACE. FOR THE BEAUTIFUL BEADS IN THESE EARRINGS, AMERICAN BEAD ARTIST NANCY PILGRIM HAS USED FUMING TO CREATE A WONDERFULLY SUBTLE GOLD COATING WITH AN ALMOST IRIDESCENT EFFECT.

TOOLS
Wire Cutters, Round-Nosed Pliers

MATERIALS
- 2 14mm rondel fumed lampwork beads
- 2 7mm gold-filled hollow seamless round beads
- 4 3mm gold-filled hollow seamless round beads
- 2 5mm gold-filled jump rings
- 2 1½" gold-filled headpins with ball tips
- 2 45mm vermeil earwires

1. Add a 3mm gold bead, a glass bead, a 7mm gold bead, and another 3mm gold bead to a headpin.

2. Cut the headpin about ⅝" above the last bead and make a wire-wrapped loop. Use the jump ring to attach this loop to the earwire.

GOLD FOIL AND GOLD EARRINGS

IN THESE BEAUTIFUL LAMPWORK "LEOPARD" BEADS BY ALENA CHLADKOVA, THE CLEAR OUTER COATING OF GLASS DISPLAYS THE INNER CORE OF PURE GOLD LEAF AND IRREGULAR BLACK GLASS "STRIPES." THE LARGE VERMEIL BEAD CAPS ARE A GOOD MATCH FOR THE INTERIOR GOLD OF THE GLASS BEAD.

TOOLS
Wire Cutters, Round-Nosed Pliers, Flat-Nosed Pliers

MATERIALS
- 2 8mm x 17.5mm rondel lampwork "tiger" beads
- 2 14mm vermeil bead caps
- 4 3mm gold-filled hollow seamless round beads
- 2 1" gold-filled headpins with ball tips
- 2 gold-filled earwires

1. Add the following elements to a headpin: a 3mm gold bead, a glass bead, a bead cap with the concave side facing the bead, and another 3mm gold bead.

2. Make a simple loop at the top of the headpin and attach it to the earwire.

GLASS AND GOLD CHAIN ADJUSTABLE NECKLACE

THIS IS A WONDERFUL WAY TO USE THE MANY EXTRA GLASS BEADS YOU WILL ACCRUE OVER TIME. IF YOU DON'T HAVE A VARIETY OF LEFTOVER BEADS, THEN AN ENTERTAINING HOUR IN A GOOD OPEN-DISPLAY BEAD STORE WILL GIVE YOU THE SELECTION YOU NEED TO MAKE THIS NECKLACE.

MANY TYPES OF GLASS BEADS ARE REPRESENTED HERE—LAMPWORK, PRESSED GLASS, DICHROIC, CRYSTAL, EVEN VINTAGE BEADS. WHEN YOU SELECT YOUR BEADS, YOU NEED ONLY TO MAKE SURE THAT THE COLOR TONES ARE SIMILAR. THE REDS AND PINKS OF THIS NECKLACE ARE PERFECTLY SUITED TO GOLD CHAIN. IF YOU PREFER TO USE SILVER CHAIN, TRY CHANGING THE COLOR TONES TO BLUES AND GREENS.

1. First, make all the dangles. For each one, select a glass bead. If the hole is a little large, use one of the 2mm or 3mm round beads, a daisy spacer, or a bead cap on the headpin. Add a spacer, a round gold bead, or both above the bead. On three of the dangles, I have used glass bead caps on top of the central bead. I have made one of the dangles with the vermeil charm by cutting the ball from the headpin, making a simple loop to hold the ring of the charm, adding a small glass bead, and finishing with another simple loop.

2. Using the jump rings, make the cluster at the end of the chain. Add one of the larger, more impressive beads to the end link of the chain; then, add two smaller dangles to the next link and two more to the link after that. If you have a double-ended component like the one in this design, cut the chain about 4" from the start and use two jump rings to join it back together with the double-ended component in between.

3. Leave another 3" of the chain empty; then, add a dangle to every other link. If you have some very small dangles, you can add them to the same links as those which already have a larger dangle—but only in a few places. Leave about 3" of chain empty after the last dangle. Add the hook clasp. To wear, simply put the hook through one of the empty links at the beginning of the necklace to create your desired length.

TOOLS
Round-Nosed Pliers, Flat-Nosed Pliers

MATERIALS

42 assorted glass beads of a red/pink or neutral color tone, from 4mm to 18mm

3   assorted glass bead caps from 10mm to 14mm

1   11mm vermeil disc charm

2   7mm silver daisy spacer beads

20 4mm vermeil daisy spacer beads

10 assorted gold-filled spacer beads

4   5mm vermeil bead caps

44 4mm gold-filled jump rings

30 3mm gold-filled hollow seamless round beads

30 2mm gold-filled round beads

1   11mm x 15mm vermeil hook clasp

42 1" gold-filled headpins with ball tips

28" of gold-filled cable chain with 6mm x 8mm links

BASIC JEWELRY MAKING

During many years as a jewelry maker, I have found that these methods work well for me. More importantly, I have found that they work well for the people I have personally taught and for the thousands of people who have been taught by our knowledgeable Beadworks instructors.

Some of these techniques are simple and require hardly any practice, although dexterity is a big help. Others need patience and several attempts to get right. If you find yourself becoming frustrated, remember that it is mostly a matter of familiarity. If at first you don't succeed, cut the beads off the thread or wire and start all over again!

There are also many bead stores and educational organizations that offer beading classes. If you are the sort of person who learns best through hands-on teaching, they provide a quick way to get started.

To begin working with beads, you need a well-lit, flat, hard surface with some kind of soft covering to stop the beads from rolling around. If you are going to work at a table or desk, you can buy bead mats or bead design boards or simply use a towel. Personally, I prefer to work on my studio floor, which is well carpeted and allows me to surround myself with tools and beads and a cat to keep me company. Have a mirror nearby so that you can check the look and length of your necklaces and earrings.

Good tools make everything a lot easier. I always use two pairs of flat-nosed pliers, one of them with narrow jaws. Your round-nosed pliers should have tips narrow enough to make really small loops. If you discover a love for making jewelry, treat yourself to a really good quality pair of wire cutters.

Once you are seriously into making jewelry, lots of little containers are essential for storing your beads and findings. These can be anything from old jars to specialized bead vials, but it does help if they are transparent and have lids. Multi-compartment plastic boxes are also a great storage method.

THE GOLDEN RULES

The carpenter's maxim is "measure twice, cut once." The wise jewelry maker measures a necklace and bracelet at least twice, and then tries it around the neck or wrist for size. She lays it down and double checks the pattern. Only then does she make the final knot or squeeze the last crimp bead shut. Never finish off your jewelry until you are absolutely sure it is right!

Don't let a little clumsy work spoil the whole piece. If you forgive a bad knot or a missed spacer, you will see the flaw every time you wear the jewelry. Better to start over and get it right.

Don't ruin good ingredients by mixing in poor ones. Even if the material is hidden by the beads or under your hair, use good quality. (Never, ever, string anything on fishing line!)

Assume you are going to make mistakes. I constantly make mistakes even after many, many years of jewelry making! If the pattern calls for two headpins, understand you will need at least two more on standby for when you cut them too short or bend them too badly. If it requires twenty inches of beading wire, make sure you have the rest of the spool nearby for when you need to start all over again.

Don't waste time looking for exactly the bead called for in a recipe. Use a substitute of the same quality with similar design values (color, size, shape, texture).

Never pass up a good bead. If you see one you really, really love, buy it, and let it inspire a future design.

I.
USING CRIMP BEADS TO ATTACH CLASPS

Crimps are little hollow tubes that can be crushed together to grip stands of beading wire. You use them like this:

1. Pass the beading wire through the crimp, then through the loop of the clasp and back through the crimp again. With a pair of crimping pliers or flat-nosed pliers, squeeze the crimp until it firmly grips both strands of the wire (Illustrations A, B).

2. Snip off the tail of the wire as close to the crimp as possible (Illustration C).

A slightly more sophisticated finish can be achieved by using crimp covers. These fit over the flattened crimp and are gently squeezed shut to create the look of a normal bead. Note though, that you can only use crimp covers if you have used crimping pliers to flatten the crimp.

Another trick is to hide the tail of the beading wire inside an adjacent bead or beads. I always do this if the hole in those beads is big enough to hold two thicknesses of beading wire, and I often add a spacer bead to the end of my design just to permit this method to be used.

1. Pass the beading wire through one or more beads, then through the crimp and through the loop of the clasp.

2. As you bring the beading wire back through the crimp, push it further back through the bead(s).

3. Squeeze the crimp shut and snip the tail of the wire as close as possible to the last bead it was passed through. In this manner, the tail end of the beading wire will recoil very slightly and be hidden inside the last bead.

A

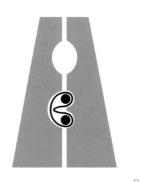 

B

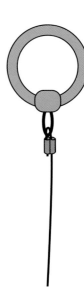

C

II.
USING JUMP RINGS AND SPLIT RINGS

JUMP RINGS

1. With a pair of flat-nosed pliers, grip the jump ring so that it lies flat between the pliers with the join slightly to one side of them.

2. Grip the other side of the join with your fingers and twist the ring sideways so that it opens.

3. After looping the ring through the piece or pieces you are connecting, close it by once again gripping it with the pliers and twisting the wire back until the two ends meet and the join is closed. Make sure that the two ends of the wire are flush with each other.

Never open jump rings by pulling the ends apart as they will be much more difficult to close. Always twist them sideways as described above.

SPLIT RINGS

1. Although there is a specialist tool you can buy to open these, the simplest way is just to slip your fingernail between the split parts of the ring just behind the opening. You should then have created enough of a space to push the piece you wish to connect into the split of the ring.

2. Rotate the ring until the connected item has traveled all the way along the split and out of the opposite side. You may want to use your flat-nosed pliers to help rotate the ring.

III.
GETTING KNOTTED:
THE ART OF USING
SILK THREAD

Strands of beads are sometimes strung on silk thread, which is thought to offer the best compromise between strength and flexibility. It is best to thread the beads onto a doubled strand of silk, both to add strength and increase the size of the knots. While you can use silk thread without knotting between each bead, it is traditional to knot between them to highlight each bead and to prevent them from chafing against each other.

STRINGING ON SILK THREAD

In order to draw the thread through the beads, you need to use a needle. While any thin needle will do, flexible twisted wire needles make the job a lot easier.

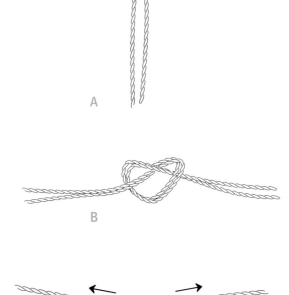

A

B

C

1. Thread the silk through the eye of the needle and draw it through until the doubled length is enough for the necklace (Illustration A). If you are knotting between each bead, your doubled strand should be at least twice as long as the finished necklace. For example, an 18" knotted necklace will require two yards or 72" of silk thread [18 x 2 x 2].
    If you are not knotting between each bead, the doubled thread should be about six inches longer than the finished piece. An 18" necklace will therefore require four feet or 48" of thread [(18 + 6) x 2].

2. Tie the doubled end of the thread with a simple overhand knot and tighten it by pulling on the tail with your pliers (Illustration B).

3. To tighten the knot even more, separate the two threads and pull apart (Illustration C).

USING AN AWL TO MAKE KNOTS:

An awl is a metal needle with a long handle that is used for getting knots to sit up tightly against beads or bead tips. It is very simple to use once you know how. You can use the next step to practice knotting. Once you begin to make a real necklace, you will first have to attach the clasp (see page 130).

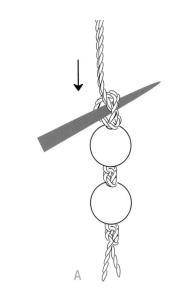

1. Add a bead to the thread. Make an overhand knot anywhere along the thread, but do not tighten it. Put the point of the awl through the knot and gently reduce the size of the knot until it fits loosely around the awl (Illustration A). Put your finger on the thread so that the knot lies between your finger and the awl.

2. Now, keeping your finger on the knot, move the awl toward the bead. You should be able to easily move the knot all the way down the thread until it is tight up against the bead.

3. Once you have the knot in position, slowly remove the awl as you pull on the thread to tighten the knot (Illustration B).

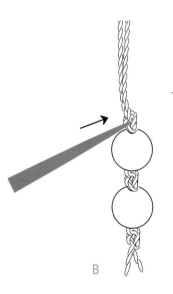

4. To tighten the knot even more, you can separate the two threads and pull apart to help force the knot closer to the bead (Illustration C).

5. Add another bead and push it firmly against the knot you have just made, then make another knot as above. Make sure the beads are tightly against one another. Continue practicing with a few beads until you are confident that you have the technique mastered.

TOOLS TIPS

When you need to knot and can't find your awl, fold out a safety pin and use that.

If you've lost your scissors or can't find your cutters, get out your nail clippers. They are usually very sharp and you can get them nice and close to your bead to cut off excess thread or wire.

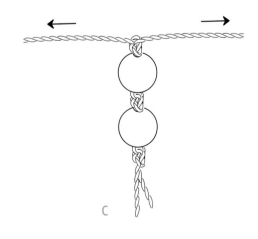

IV.
USING BEAD TIPS TO ATTACH CLASPS

When you are stringing on silk thread, you need to finish off the ends in a way that will let you attach them to each half of a clasp. The little findings that enable you to do this are called bead tips. One end of a bead tip is a simple loop that will connect to the clasp. The other end grips the knot at the end of your thread.

To use either kind of bead tip, start with your thread doubled and knotted at the end.

STRING-THROUGH "CLAMSHELL" BEAD TIPS

1. Start with your doubled thread knotted at the end. Make another overhand knot on top of the first knot at the end of your thread. This is easier to do if you use your awl to guide the loop of the second knot to a point where it will sit on the first. Tighten that knot as well. Unless you are very sure of your knots, add a dab of hypo-cement or clear nail varnish. Trim off the excess tail of the thread with a pair of sharp scissors (Illustrations A, B, C, D).

2. Pass your needle and thread into the open clamshell of the bead tip and through the hole at the base of the shell. Pull the thread completely through so that the knot sits snugly inside the clamshell. Using flat-nosed pliers, gently squeeze the sides of the shell together so that it closes around the knot and grips it firmly (Illustrations E, F).

3. Make another single knot tightly against the bottom of the bead tip. Now add the beads to the silk thread to create your necklace.

4. Once you have completed stringing all the beads of your necklace, finish it off by passing the needle and thread through the hole on the outside of another bead tip. (Remember to make a knot after the last bead.)

5. Pull the thread so that the last knot of your necklace sits firmly against the outside of the bead tip. Now tie an overhand knot so that it sits inside the clamshell of the bead tip. To position the knot properly, use your awl to move the loop of the knot as close to the inside wall of the bead tip as possible, then tighten the knot, pulling the awl out at the last moment. Make a second overhand knot and tighten it on top of the first. Add a dab of hypo-cement if needed. Using flat-nosed pliers, gently squeeze the sides of the shell together so that it closes around the knot and grips it firmly.

6. Using a sharp pair of scissors, trim off the rest of the thread as close to the outside of the bead tip as possible.

7. You now have a strand with a bead tip at either end. Put the open loop of one bead tip through the ring on one half of the clasp. Use flat-nosed pliers to close the loop so that it is firmly attached to the ring. Attach the other bead tip to the other part of the clasp in the same manner.

TIP

If you add a few smaller beads to the beginning and end of your necklace, it will be easier to open and undo the clasp when you wear it.

QUICK TRICK

If you have an idea for a necklace but don't have the time to make it up, string a few beads defining at least part of the design on a piece of thread or even fishing line and tie off both ends. This way you will be able to remember what the idea was when you find time to make it.

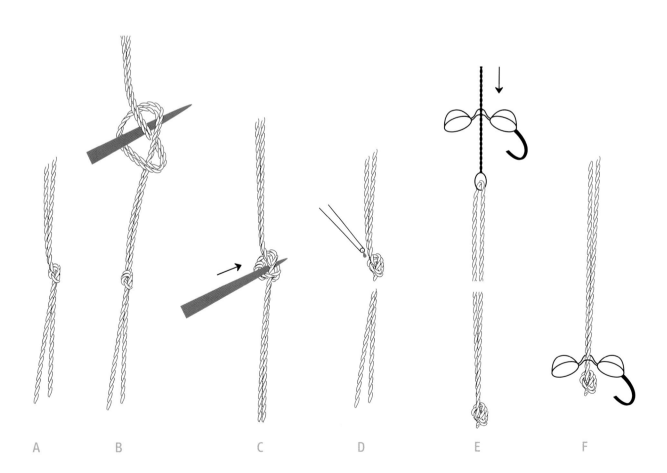

A   B   C   D   E   F

USING "BASKET" BEAD TIPS

While it is a little more difficult to make the final knot in this style of bead tip, they give a more sophisticated look to your jewelry—if you can master the technique.

1. Take the end of the doubled thread and tie a simple overhand knot. Tighten it by gripping the tail with pliers and pulling. Trim off the excess tail of the thread with a pair of sharp scissors (Illustration A).

2. Pass your needle and thread into the inside of the "basket" and through the hole at the bottom. Pull the thread completely through so that the knot sits snugly inside the bottom of the basket. Put a tiny dab of hypo-cement or clear nail polish on the knot (Illustrations B, C, D).

3. Make another overhand knot near the outside of the bead tip and use your awl to move the loop of that knot tight against the bottom of the "basket." This knot will prevent the beads from chafing against the bead tip and improve the overall appearance.

4. Now add the beads on to the silk thread to create your necklace (Illustration E).

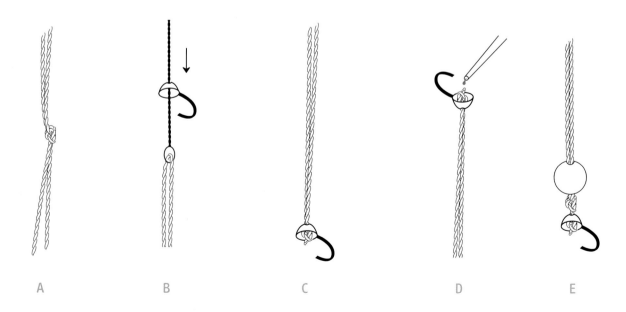

A   B   C   D   E

5. Once you have completed stringing all the beads of your
    necklace, make an overhand knot and use the awl to position
    it tightly against the last bead. Now pass the needle and thread
    through the hole on the outside bottom of another basket bead
    tip. Pull the thread until the bead tip sits firmly against the
    knot after the last bead (Illustration F).

6. Now tie an overhand knot and use your awl to move the loop
    of the knot as close as possible to the bottom inside wall of the
    bead tip (Illustration G), then tighten the knot, pulling the awl
    out at the last moment. It takes a little practice to get this final
    knot to slip into the "basket," but it is important to get a good
    tight fit so that no thread can be seen once the necklace is
    complete. Add a tiny dab of hypo-cement or clear nail polish
    to this knot (Illustration H).

7. Finish off by attaching the ends of the bead tips to the clasp as
    above (Illustrations I, J).

F   G   H   I   J

V.
USING HEADPINS
AND EYEPINS

Headpins and eyepins are convenient ways of attaching beads to necklaces, earwires, and other findings. Simply add some beads and make a loop at the top. To make the loop:

1. Hold the bottom of the pin to make sure the beads are sitting tightly against it, and cut the top of the pin to the correct length for the loop. For a 3mm size loop, there should be a quarter of an inch of the pin above the last bead. Small loops are made by gripping the wire towards the tips of the plier's jaws. If you grip the wire further back, the loop will be larger. If the loop is bigger, you must allow more wire between the bead and the end of the pin. When you practice this technique, it is useful to make a mark on the jaws of your round-nosed pliers so that you know where to place the wire between the jaws (Illustration A).

2. Grip the top of the pin between the jaws of round-nosed pliers. Make a "P" shape by rolling the pliers away from you. Move the pliers around if necessary until the tip of the pin meets the wire at the top of the bead (Illustration B).

3. Put your fingernail behind the neck of the "P" where it touches the bead, and bend the loop back until it is centered above the bead. Your finished loop should look like a balloon with the string hanging straight down (Illustration C).

4. To attach the loop to another, open it to the side as with the jump ring below.

NOTE

If you are wire wrapping on a headpin or eyepin, follow the instructions on page 135, substituting the headpin or eyepin for the wire. For larger loops, allow more distance on the wire. Remember the wire's placement on the jaws of your pliers determines the size of your loop.

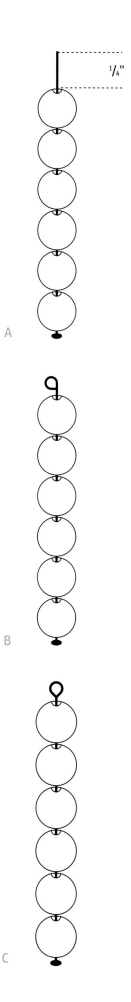

A

B

C

¼"

VI.
WIRE WRAPPING

This technique can be used with precious metal and other wires or with headpins and eyepins. It forms a stronger loop and adds a space between the loop and the bead. This is a technique that you need to practice many times to master. To create a small wire wrapped loop at each end of a bead:

1. Cut a piece of wire which is the width of the bead plus about 1$\frac{1}{2}$" (Illustration A).

2. With round-nosed pliers, grip the wire about $\frac{1}{2}$" from the end. Bend the wire around the pliers until a loop is formed and the tail of the wire is perpendicular to the stem (Illustration B).

3. With your fingernail behind the loop, use the pliers to roll it back until it is centered above the stem of the wire (Illustration C).

4. Using your finger or fingernail, wrap the tail of the wire around the stem a couple of turns. Use flat-nosed pliers to finish wrapping the tail tightly. If there is any excess wire, snip it off (Illustrations D and E).

5. Place a bead on the wire. Grip the wire so that the jaws are about $\frac{3}{8}$" from the bead and roll the pliers until a loop is formed and the tail of the wire is perpendicular to the stem (Illustrations F and B).

6. With your fingernail behind the loop, roll it back until it is centered above the stem of the wire (Illustration C).

7. Using your finger or fingernail, wrap the tail of the wire around the stem a couple of turns, getting tightly between the bead and the loop Use flat-nosed pliers to finish wrapping the tail tightly. Snip off any excess wire (Illustrations D, E).

NOTE
When making a single loop on a headpin or eyepin, cut the wire about $\frac{5}{8}$" above the bead when making a medium-sized loop.

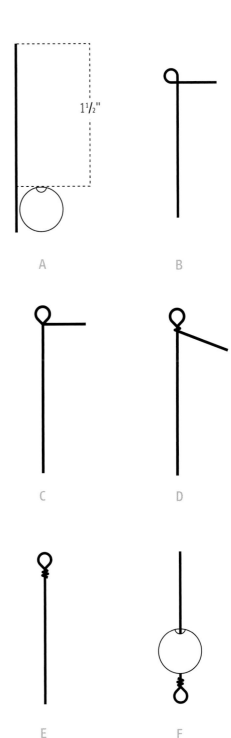

1$\frac{1}{2}$"

A

B

C

D

E

F

STANDARD MEASUREMENTS

BEAD SIZES

The diameter of beads is commonly described in millimeters. Since you often need to work out how many beads to buy for a particular length, it is useful to know how many beads there are per inch. It's especially useful to know how many beads are in sixteen inches, that being one of the typical lengths of temporarily strung beads. The chart to the right shows you the number per inch of some common sizes of round beads.

Seed beads, however, are a strange exception to the sensible practice of sizing in millimeters. They are, instead, classified by an arcane system that seems to have originated in the nineteenth century in the Czech city of Gablonz. Despite the fact that it is neither very useful nor very consistent, the system has persisted. The reference point starts with a medium-sized glass bead, which has a value of zero. A bead somewhat smaller would have two zeros; one smaller yet, three zeros, and so on. Because very tiny beads have many zeros, it is easier to write them as a number like so: 11/0, meaning the bead is eleven zeros, or eleven sizes smaller than the "zero" reference bead. What makes this system awkward is that the beads with the higher numbers are smaller than the beads with the smaller ones; thus, a 13/0 seed bead is much smaller than an 8/0 seed bead. The situation is even more confusing because Czech standards and Japanese standards vary slightly—the size refers only to the diameter of the bead, not to the width. Keeping in mind that there are differences between different manufacturers' standards, as well as that the widths of individual seed beads often vary, the chart shown at right can be used as a rough guide to their sizes.

APPROXIMATE NUMBER OF ROUND BEADS

Bead Size	1"	7"	16"	18"
2 mm	12	88	200	225
3 mm	8	59	134	150
4 mm	6	44	100	114
5 mm	5	35	80	90
6 mm	4	29	67	76
7 mm	3.5	25	58	65
8 mm	3	22	50	57
9 mm	2.5	19	45	40
10 mm	2.5	17	40	45
12 mm	2	14	33	38

Seed Bead Size	Approximate diameter in millimeters	Approximate number of beads in an inch
15/0	1.4 to 1.5 mm	32 to 35
13/0	1.6 to 1.7 mm	24 to 27
11/0	2.0 to 2.1 mm	18 to 19
8/0	3.0 to 3.1 mm	11 to 12
11/0	2.0 to 2.1 mm	18 to 19
8/0	3.0 to 3.1 mm	11 to 12
6/0	4.0 mm	8 to 9

LENGTH CONVERSIONS:

1 inch = 25.4 millimeters

1 foot = 0.3 meter

1 millimeter = 0.04 inch

1 meter = 3.3 foot

BUYING BEADS

Since glass beads occupy one of the major roles on the jewelry stage, a bead store should devote considerable space to their display. At a minimum, there should be a range of seed, pressed-glass, lampwork, and crystal beads, as well as some antique, vintage, and contemporary beads. As I have recommended in this book, do not become fixated on buying exactly the bead described in a particular materials list. The variety of beads is just so enormous that bead stores can only carry a small part of the whole. You will usually find a bead that is similar to the one you seek; any variation in color or pattern will only add to the unique character of your jewelry.

Allowing for similar substitutions, a good bead store should provide you with a variety of precious-metal findings and spacer beads sufficient to make any of the designs in this book. That selection should include seamless hollow rounds in several sizes, other spacer beads, and individual beads of character. All silver beads should be of sterling fineness (925) or higher. Gold beads can take a little more effort to acquire, but many stores carry a range of vermeil and gold-filled beads.

Although nothing beats seeing and touching the beads directly, there are now many online bead sellers who have invested heavily in providing excellent images of their beads and easy systems for purchasing them. Online auctions, mail-order catalogs, and bead magazines all provide sources for acquiring beads from a distance. On the Internet you can also explore the Web pages of many contemporary glass bead artists, as well as see some of their truly remarkable lampwork glass bead creations. You should be able to find just about anything you want from the comfort of your own armchair—a far cry from the days when a search for beads meant long, often fruitless hours trudging around commercial bead districts.

WIRE THICKNESS
Beading Wires

Since the width of bead holes is expressed in millimeters, you might expect that the wires that fit through them are sized in the same way. Unfortunately, most beading wire widths are measured in inches. The following conversion chart is helpful if you know the size of the bead hole.

0.021 in. = 0.53mm
0.018 in. = 0.45mm
0.015 in. = 0.38mm
0.013 in. = 0.33mm

PRECIOUS METAL WIRES

While beading wire thicknesses are at least measured in inches, precious metal wires can be measured in American standard gauge, in inches, or in millimeters. Confusingly, the higher the gauge number, the thinner the wire. The chart below helps sort it out.

18 gauge = 0.0403 in. = 1.02mm
20 gauge = 0.0320 in. = 0.81mm
22 gauge = 0.0253 in. = 0.64mm
24 gauge = 0.0201 in. = 0.51mm
26 gauge = 0.0159 in. = 0.40mm
28 gauge = .0126 in. = 0.32mm

RESOURCES

Most of the materials used in this book are available at fine beading stores everywhere. You can find many of them at Beadworks stores and at www.beadworks.com.

There are several internet directories of bead stores including:

www.guidetobeadwork.com

www.mapmuse.com
This website quickly finds a bead store location near you if you go to "hobbies and crafts" and then to "beading shops."

A number of publications serve the beading community and have large resource listings:
Bead Style Magazine
www.beadstylemag.com
Beadwork Magazine
www.interweave.com/bead/beadwork_magazine

For information about Swarovski Crystal products:
www.create-your-style.com

There are many wonderful glass bead artists who have their works exhibited online with details about where to find them:
Alena and Alex Chladkova, www.aleale.cz
Leah Fairbanks, www.leahfairbanks.com
Kate Fowle Meleney, www.katefowle.com
Kristen Frantzen Orr, www.kristenfrantzenorr.com
Susan Knopp, www.susanknoppenamels.com
Kevin O'Grady, www.kevinogrady.com
Nancy Pilgrim, www.nancypilgrim.com
Cynthia Liebler Saari, www.clsaari.com
Bruce St John Maher, www.maherglass.com

Due to the rapid growth of bead stores over the last twenty years, there is now a wide selection of places to buy beads, findings, and threading materials. In North America alone, there are far more than a thousand bead stores, as well as dozens of online retailers. While shopping online can be quick and convenient, nothing beats the experience of going to a well-stocked bead store. There you are able to feel the texture of the beads and arrange them side by side to see whether the combinations please you.

If you are inspired by the designs in this book but are too busy to make them yourself, visit www.NancyAlden.com for a range of finished jewelry.

ACKNOWLEDGMENTS

The jewelry in this book was designed and created by Nancy Alden.

I would like to thank all the glass bead designers who have provided jewelry makers like me with the essential elements of our design. Each one of the millions of glass bead designs was the work of some individual artisan; the names of most of them are unknown. In the last few decades, a few contemporary bead makers have become acknowledged masters of their art and been properly credited for their work. We are happy to have had the opportunity to recommend their fine designs in some of the projects in this book. In particular, I would like to thank Alena Chladkova for her bright and youthful creations which have reinvigorated the designs of the Czech glass bead industry and provided much inspiration for my own glass bead jewelry.

Thanks also to the following people for their work on the book:
Jennifer Lévy, photography
Lindsay Bartlett, jewelry model
Liz Doughty and Ivannia Gomez, jewelry components coordinators
Stephen Sammons, research
Everyone at Potter Craft including Rosy Ngo, Chi Ling Moy, Courtney Conroy, and Amy Sly.

I dedicate this book to my sons, Nicholas and Christopher, who, being boys, have absolutely no interest in my beads and jewelry, and bring, therefore, a proper sense of balance to my life.

ABOUT THE AUTHOR

Nancy Alden is a jewelry designer and cofounder of the Beadworks Group, one of the world's largest retailers of beads. As Beadworks' principal buyer and designer, she travels the world in search of the most beautiful components for jewelry design. She is as at home with gemstone merchants in Jaipur, silver makers in Bali, and glass artists in Bohemia as she is with pearl producers in China. Her knowledge of beads and findings is unrivaled, spanning all categories of material and all stages of production from the creation of a single bead to its final role in a finished piece of jewelry.

Starting as a silver and goldsmith, Nancy turned to designing with beads because of the vastly greater possibilities for creative expression. Having seen the world of jewelry design open for herself, she then went on to introduce other people to the creative pleasures and the economies of making their own jewelry. By creating Beadworks classes and sharing her skills with other instructors, she has generated a network of teachers who have added to the ever-growing number of women and men able to design and create jewelry. When she is not in search of new beads, Nancy divides her time between her home in Connecticut and her studio retreats in Europe and the Grenadines.

ABOUT BEADWORKS

In 1978, a small store in London began selling a very ancient product in a very novel way. Although beads are among the very earliest of traded articles, the concept of offering a large, sophisticated, and open display to the general public was new.

The shop never advertised—indeed, it didn't even have a name for many years—but the demand for its products was immediate and overwhelming. Simply by word of mouth, the original store became world famous.

With American jewelry designer, Nancy Alden, the concept expanded to North America, where it has grown to half a dozen stores and a mail-order business. Beadworks has inspired people from around the world to open their own bead stores, enabling hundreds of thousands of people to make their own jewelry. You can visit Beadworks online at www.beadworks.com.

INDEX

Page numbers in *italics* indicate illustrations.